HOW TO CREATE A NEW IDENTITY

D1502897

HOW TO CREATE A NEW IDENTITY

BY ANONYMOUS

CITADEL PRESS
SECAUCUS, N.J.

Published by Citadel Press
A division of Lyle Stuart Inc.
120 Enterprise Ave., Secaucus, N.J. 07094
In Canada: Musson Book Company
A division of General Publishing Co. Limited
Don Mills, Ontario

Previously published under the title *New I.D. in America: How to Create a Foolproof New Identity* by Paladin Press.

Manufactured in the United States of America

ISBN 0-8065-1034-X

5 6 7 8 9 10

CONTENTS

INTRODUCTION

One need not be planning to kill Charles DeGaulle, as was the assassin in *The Day of the Jackal,* to take advantage of a false identity. The applications are countless, limited only by one's imagination.

People create new identities for numerous reasons. Income taxes can be avoided, as can the obligations of an old life, such as spouse support, burdensome debts, and legal judgments; driving records stay clean so insurance rates are lowest; service of process for lawsuits can be avoided; if arrested and jailed, bail can be made and a falsely identified party can disappear without ever being heard from again; underage teens needing to drive or wanting to drink can utilize such an identity; immigrants, tired of fighting the immigration department, can become instant citizens; clear passports for travel in or out of the United States can be obtained; business fronts can be set up, complete with bank accounts; and new grade "A" credit can be gained while negative credit references can be eliminated and the consequences avoided.

These are only a few examples. The applications are as varied as the individuals who have in the past taken advantage of the information presented in this book.

Misconceptions abound about what constitutes a false identity. Information is readily available that shows how to create or obtain phony, and I might add crude, imitations of valid documents. What I show you are the best ways of obtaining various types of functional identifying documentation, including birth certificates, drivers' licenses, passports, social security cards, employment records, credit cards, and other items needed to prove and become a new person. Furthermore, not only does this book contain information on how to become a new person, for whatever reasons, but also how to erase your past completely.

Another misconception is that you either create a complete identity from the ground up or not at all. This is totally incorrect. There are varying degrees of identity development, various stages if you will, depending upon the needs of the user. You may simply want to obtain a state-issued I.D. card, and this is quite easy enough. On the other hand, you may need to create a totally new "paper individual" while at the same time eliminating all traces of the "old you." Perhaps your needs lie somewhere in between. The choice is yours and yours alone.

Many people lead normal lives, utilizing false identities. They oftentimes live under their real identity and only use the false identity on special occasions. One example of this is a former client of mine who was tired of getting traffic tickets under his real name. His solution was to drive under his alternative I.D. and when pulled over, use this paper person to receive the ticket. Another former client is in a business where lawsuits are standard operating procedure. To avoid service of process, he merely shows the process server an alternative piece of I.D. identifying him as someone other than his true self, and the confused process server can merely shrug his shoulders, walk away, and attempt to look further for the target of his bad news.

The important thing to remember is that the time is *now* if you need or feel you might need one, or a number of new identities. Once a good identity is created, it is always good and can be stored away for future use. Generally, the laws in the fifty states provide no penalty for creating a new identity. But who knows how long this windfall will last, for the government's ability and apparent need to keep tabs on its citizens increases with every new day.

What I intend to show you, drawing upon eighteen years' experience as a private investigator employed primarily to seek out missing persons and hide those who do not want to be found, is how to lose yourself from people like me, and any other legal, quasi-legal or outright illegal agency that is interested in finding you. What you will be doing if you choose to create a new person is much the same as government people do when they hide an informer from the retribution of his "friends." Under the Witness Security Program, they give such people a fresh, safe start by issuing them a new, valid U.S. identity. The only difference between what they do and what you can do is that the government is not authorizing (and most importantly won't know about) your doing the same thing.

Over the years, I have created over two hundred forms of new I.D. for my various clients, and relocated hundreds of persons trying to hide under varying degrees of poorly-designed identity alterations. The main reason they could be relocated is because they had utilized incorrect or incomplete information in creating their new identity. By discovering just one thread unraveled, the good investigator can eventually find his subject, and believe me, if an investigator, who in reality is just a private citizen, can do it, the government, with all its resources, can do it, too. During this time, I have personally utilized at least fifteen identities and traveled under seven different passports. The point is, identity alteration can be done repeatedly and is not necessarily a one-shot deal.

You are about to read through information that has made me tens of thousands of dollars over the course of my career. As far as our government is concerned, I am a good taxpaying citizen. I own income real estate and have numerous investments. For all intents and purposes, I am secure. But what gives me the most security, what I believe to be *absolute security*, lies quietly in my safe deposit box: a large quantity of cash, gold bullion, valuable gem stones, and two complete and virgin sets of I.D., including passports and credit cards. This to me is security. For in an increasingly Big Brother-type society, where governments all over the world spend enormous amounts of time and money assuring themselves the masses will not step out of line, I will always have my freedom.

1. YOU ARE WHO YOU SAY YOU ARE

This chapter contains perhaps the most important information in the whole book. While anyone can get legal U.S. documentation in another name as the ensuing chapters detail, the information contained in the chapter "You Are Who You Say You Are" is essential to know and use throughout and well beyond alternative identity development. The thrust of this chapter is that you must totally become the person your identification "proves" you to be. You must not only develop sound documentation, but also the proper mental attitude to most effectively utilize an alternative identity.

False or alternative identities work extraordinarily well, and altogether most effectively, when the two mutually dependent aspects of form and substance are taken into account. This is to say that one cannot only externally, through documentation, become someone new (form), but must also internally become that new person (substance). This is by no means as hard to accomplish as it sounds. It is another way of saying that you have to look and play the part as well as learn the lines. One of the most simple yet effective private investigator's tricks substantiates this theory. This merely consists of printing up a business card (form) identifying yourself as required and acting out the part (substance).

More on Form

What has always surprised me is how simple it is to establish valid United States documentation under an assumed name and how much people rely on that piece of plastic or paper that says "I am John Doe." This is the form people are so easily convinced by. You would be amazed at how many times I have flashed a five-and-dime badge in a person's eyes explaining I was a police investigator, and that person, without even questioning me, would willingly divulge the most sensitive information!

One of the reasons the use of valid documentation and an assumed name works so easily is that this is one of the few countries in the world that does not have one unique national document, easily scrutinized, to identify the bearer. Consequently, documents not initially intended to serve as standardized I.D. are used as such in every state. The advantages of this system to you are obvious.

Take a state driver's license for example. In every state the document differs, yet it is valid in every other state. Some have thumbprints, some photographs; some are plastic and look like credit cards, while others are merely paper. Additionally, states differ with respect to what they require to issue a driver's license. All this is due to the fact that the driver's license originated as a way for the state to insure your driving capability and not to prove your identity. The beneficial side effect is that this easily obtained document is accepted everywhere as proof of who you are.

Our society's blind faith in paper proof of identity is really a condition of history. In the smaller community atmosphere of the past, it was possible to readily verify a person's background. Today, because of the increasingly complex nature of society, things have changed. In today's fast-paced, overpopulated world, people cannot take the time or incur the expense to investigate the background of another, and even if they would like to, few have the capabilities. As a consequence, an enormous, almost unfathomable degree of trust in documentation exists in our society. When a man hands you his calling card saying he is the president of a corporation or a doctor, the natural and most practical thing to do is believe him until he gives you a reason not to.

This basic need to trust works on all levels. An example is a client of mine who made himself a multimillionaire importing marijuana. His requirements were a complete alternative identity to live under while transacting business. When arrested, all the police had to go on was his valid alternative identification, the corroborating information he provided them with, and the fingerprints (which in many jurisdictions are conveniently referenced only by name, not identifying characteristics). The net effect was that my client, merely figuring the loss as business expense, paid his bail money and disappeared from the face of the earth, only to rise again as another person.

The end result is that short of an extensive background check, few people are ever checked out on even the most fundamental level. And, as will be seen, even the most extensive background check can be circumvented. Any good con man will tell you that people want to trust other people. This obviously works to the distinct advantage of a person passing himself off as someone he is not.

More on Substance

Having a pocketful of new identity, including driver's license, credit cards, passport and the like, is easy, inexpensive and fascinating, but it is not everything. As mentioned earlier, substance, the way you as an individual play the game, is the other half of the equation. In other words, alternative identity seekers must learn to internally become the person or profession that externally they are professing to be. If you are approached by someone with a three-day growth of beard, ragged tennis shoes and dirty fingernails who hands you a business card identifying himself as a broker on the New York Stock Exchange, you would tend not to believe him. The reason is that after a review of his perfect documentation (form), the external sources (substance) indicate that this individual does not fit your preconceived notion of what a stock broker should look like. But, if that same person came up to you in a three-piece suit, gold watch chain, polished shoes, and clean fingernails, you would tend to believe him because the form and substance would fit.

There is also an advantageous intimidation factor involved. It is one thing to question a bum, but another to question a person of obvious status. Ironically, in many situations, even if one's alternative identity papers are lacking in some way, the combined factors of looking and talking the part often carry him through. Any investigator will admit that the intimidation of simply appearing as people expect you to under the circumstances can do more than any amount of paper work. Together, a valid alternative identity and proper mental attitude provide an impenetrable false identity.

2. SETTING THE CORNERSTONE

The cornerstone of all identity is the birth certificate. It is the most widely accepted form of identification in the United States. Theoretically, every citizen has a piece of paper which identifies him at birth, along with the state of birth, the mother, father, and often the hospital where the birth occurred. If a person is born in a hospital, at home, or in the back of a 1957 Chevrolet, he receives some type of certification that identifies him. The document could be a certificate of live birth which is prepared in a hospital when they have direct evidence that a child was born at that place. It could be a certificate of delayed birth, which is often utilized when a person did not receive a certificate of live birth for reasons as varied as delivery at home or destruction of the original certificate. Regardless of the type of certificate, the birth record document is the most requested document when applying for other necessary identification such as a driver's license or passport. It is the foundation document for a person's identity and as we shall see, surprisingly simple to produce.

Birth certificates are almost as varied as the people who possess them. They have no photographs and rarely finger or footprints. Sometimes they have an embossed stamp, can be multiple colors or almost any size, and can be valid even if they are reduced photocopies and simply stamped "Certified."

The only really consistent aspect is that they are invariably signed by a doctor or hospital administrator. In short, there are various types of birth certificates in circulation and most are almost comically simple documents. The net result is that it is basically impossible for any one person to have seen them all or to be able to say that a particular certificate is not real simply because of its design or layout.

The Birth Certificate—Two Ways of Getting One

There are two methods commonly used to obtain a birth certificate in another name. One is the counterfeit-forgery method, the other is commonly referred to as the infant death method. Each method is unique and its utilization depends entirely upon the reason for which one is establishing a false identity. Each method works equally well for its intended purpose. I define them for simplicity's sake as the short-term and long-term methods because of the period of effective utilization. As will be seen, there are advantages to each.

Counterfeit-Forgery (Short-Term)

The counterfeit-forgery method can be used to obtain all the valid identification that is discussed in later chapters, except for a passport. This method is simple, effective, and takes little time to complete.

The advantages of creating a new identity or identities by utilization of the counterfeit-forgery method are obvious. First, it is easy to establish and therefore, it is easy to discard that "person" and create another. Second, one can pick the name he or she might want to use.

Forging a birth certificate involves taking a valid

document and altering or changing the information within its four corners. One easy and effective method for obtaining blank birth certificate forms is to purchase them as hospitals often do from a document supply company. This can be done either by telephone or in person, but you must establish yourself as a legitimate purchaser as every supplier has a different sales' policy. However, even when a supplier with a restrictive policy is encountered, a good imagination, along with form and substance, will turn him into a ready seller. For example, if I were to call a supplier, I might identify myself as the administrator of "Acme Hospital" looking for a new supplier of forms. I could then request a copy of their catalog containing examples of birth certificates and perhaps certificates of live birth. Once received, orders can be placed directly. Under this circumstance, I would always have a mailing address (see Chapter 6) established under the name of the fictitious hospital to receive the documents. Many times this is particularly effective if you call a supplier in a smaller city and have the documents sent to your "hospital" address in a larger city. I have also found that the greater the distance between the supplier and the purchaser, the more legitimate the transaction appears to the supplier. I don't know why this unusual quirk of human psychology occurs, but experience has shown me over and over again that it is indeed a reality.

Another method is to personally visit the supplier's store, as the same administrator mentioned above. Have a card from the hospital printed up with your fictitious name. From that point, you merely present it to the sales person, and purchase the supplies you require.

An alternative and much favored method of obtaining birth certificate blanks is to alter an existing birth certificate. This involves getting a printer to reproduce a

real birth certificate, excluding any of the original typewritten birth data on it. In other words, the printer
creates a new blank birth certificate from an actual
legal original. With the advent of modern printing
techniques, print shops of sufficient skill are available
in almost every town. Some printers would do this for
you without even thinking twice. However, under some
circumstances, a printer would hesitate in taking on this
job even for a customer paying in cash. It is then up to
you to once again utilize your imagination. For example, you might innocently explain to the printer that
it is your parents' twenty-fifth wedding anniversary and
you, as well as your brothers and sisters in other cities,
are preparing a very special, personal gift for them. Explain that the gift is a unique reproduction of each
offspring's birth certificate. The intent is to have a
printer clean-up the certificates, i.e., take off all the
typewritten material, so that the certificate is like
new. The certificates are then going to be sent to a cal-
ligrapher so that the blanks can be completed in fancy
script, making a very beautiful gift indeed. Once completed, your story continues, the children intend to
frame the new documents and present them to their
parents as an anniversary present. Done properly, this
story could bring tears to the printer's eyes.

Basically, he then has a reason to take off all the
superfluous data while leaving the certificate form blank
and intact. Leave the doctor's signature if you want, or
have it taken off for resignature later. The printer will
then photograph the document, remove the unwanted
information from the negative with chemicals, and make
a plate to reproduce the new negative. Be sure to have
the printer print both sides of the new certificate if
the original has printing on both sides, and get extra
copies.

Another example of how I have gotten printers to do the job is by explaining that I was a film producer in need of a blank birth certificate as a film prop. During one special scene in the movie, the camera will pan the birth certificate, which will be filled in by the studio art department to fit the needs of the film.

A third method for obtaining a blank certificate is one I recommend only for investigators or the truly desperate. It is one of the oldest and most risky methods known and has been shown on almost every private eye television show. Find someone in your city or county bureau of vital statistics, hall of records, or whatever it is called in your city, and bribe that person for a blank birth certificate.

Completing the Document

It is hard to imagine an adult applying for a driver's license with a brand-new, fresh-looking birth certificate not giving rise to suspicion. An original birth certificate has usually been folded and filed in a book, drawer or safe deposit box for any number of years and evidences its age by virtue of its color and texture as well as data. These are important considerations in completing a blank document.

It is more than likely, depending on the user's age, that highly efficient electric typewriters were not available at the time the birth certificate would have been completed. Therefore, it is inadvisable to fill out the certificate with a modern IBM Selectric typewriter, but instead an old-fashioned manual typewriter should be sought out from the attic, old pawn shop, government office, or public library. It is also likely that ball point pens were not in use at the time of birth, so in signing the document, a fountain pen should be utilized. While most of these details, even if ignored, can go unnoticed, attention to them helps make this procedure virtually foolproof.

Aging the document is most important. Most aging can be accomplished in a relatively short period of time simply by leaving the certificate in the sunshine. Another more efficient method is that practiced by the more renowned art forgers when they are aging their canvases. The procedure involves submersing the blank certificates in tea solution until the desired tone is obtained, and thereafter allowing them to dry. The dried certificates can be folded and unfolded until the paper achieves the look of an old, roughly handled document.

An alternative to aging the document is the certified copy method. Normally, when a person's birth certificate is lost, a copy can be obtained from the Bureau of Vital Statistics or the equivalent agency in the city where the individual was born. What the Bureau of Vital Statistics provides is a copy of the original document of birth filed by the hospital, which is certified upon request for an additional fee. It is important to note that certification is what authenticates the copy. These certified copies can take many forms. The certificate is often microstatted or photocopied on a larger piece of paper to which a certified stamp is then affixed. While every county certifies documents, the form of this certification stamp varies. Certification stamps look different, and the method of application often differs. Therefore, like the birth certificate itself, it is extremely difficult for anyone examining a certified copy to judge whether it has been done officially. The net result is that regardless of the procedure used, the only uniform characteristic is the look and feel of authenticity.

Any document can be certified. If you want an example of a particular agency's certification, you need only to mail or hand deliver a document to the county

NEW YORK STATE DEPARTMENT OF HEALTH
OFFICE OF VITAL STATISTICS
ALBANY

CERTIFICATE OF BIRTH REGISTRATION

This is to certify that a birth certificate has been filed for

_____

Born on _____ , at _____

Son of _____ and
(name of father)

_____
(maiden name of mother)

Date Filed _____
Local Registrar

THIS CERTIFICATE IS EVIDENCE OF AGE, PARENTAGE AND PLACE OF BIRTH AND SHOULD BE CAREFULLY PRESERVED
When the child is vaccinated against smallpox and inoculated against diphtheria or any other disease, ask the physician or clinic to fill in the
spaces below.

Vaccinated against smallpox _____

Inoculated against diphtheria _____

Inoculated against whooping cough _____

Inoculated against tetanus _____

Birth Certificate—Front

IMPORTANT NOTICE TO PARENTS

This certificate of birth registration is evidence that the birth of your child has been officially registered. You should preserve it because it is legal evidence of age and citizenship.

Please check the accuracy of date, place of birth, and spelling of names. If you find an error, inform the local registrar at once. A correction made now will prevent the possibility of complications later.

The original record of your child's birth will be permanently preserved in the office of the State Department of Health at Albany. A *complete copy* of the birth certificate is on file in the office of the local registrar of the community in which your child was born.

If the child was not named at the time the birth was recorded, a special supplemental report form should accompany this certificate. Please enter the child's given name on this report as soon as possible and return it together with the certificate to the local registrar, requesting him to make out a new certificate of registration containing the child's given name.

Form V. S. 66. 5-20-53-100M (3A-261)

EXTRACTS FROM THE VITAL
STATISTICS LAW

§382. The birth of each and every child born in this state shall be registered within five days after the date of each birth***.

§384. When any certificate of birth of a living child is presented without the statement of the given name, the local registrar shall make out and deliver to the parents of the child a special blank for the supplemental report of the given name of the child, which shall be filled out as directed, and returned to the local registrar as soon as the child shall have been named. The given name, supplied by the supplemental report, shall be entered on the original birth certificate.

§389. ***Within ten days after receiving the certificate of birth he (the local registrar) shall furnish without charge to the parents or guardian of the child or to the mother at the address designated by her for the purpose, a certificate of registration, to be made out on a form furnished by the state commissioner of health***.

Birth Certificate—Back

clerk, local courthouse, or wherever they certify documents in that county, and ask to have the document stamped "Certified." Upon return, you then have an example of what certified copies look like for that area. You can then have a similar stamp or embosser manufactured like the original. It is important to remember that you are simply making the document look official. Therefore, any certification you make can be applied to the document and will invariably work.

Certifying a document yourself is simple. It involves either a stamp, an embossing, or both. Most printers who make stamps and round embossers will make what you need. Have the printer make an official-looking certified stamp with a blank line beneath the word "Certified" so that a signature, allegedly of a clerk, can be filled in. Also have a round embossing seal prepared with fancy scrollwork with the word "Certified." If one is particularly detail oriented, the name of the respective county can be included on the stamp and embosser. Then, stamp your document, initial it, and emboss over the stamp. The document then looks and feels official and is easily accepted. An alternative method is to use any embosser, regardless of what it says, and only partially stamp the certificate. The embossed portion is raised, and can then be felt, so it seems official, but it is impossible to read. Therefore it cannot be exposed as a fake.

You can even manufacture these certification stamps by purchasing a rubber stamp that allows you to fill in the letters and words you want. These changeable rubber stamps can be purchased at almost any good stationery supply store and are always useful because of their variability. Even rub-off letter appliques can be useful, and when photocopied look excellent on a document.

Conclusion

The most important element in applying any information in this book, including the counterfeit-forgery birth certificate method, is preparation. You must be like the finest trial lawyers and never put yourself in a situation where you do not already know the outcome. In that way, you are never surprised.

This too is the private investigator's most valuable tool and a necessary lesson to learn if one wants to formulate a new identity. For example, your printer may tell you that he cannot prepare the birth certificate because while you (well-dressed and obviously a person of substance and good intent) would not consider using a blank certificate for illegal purposes, some other person, less scrupulous, could get his hands on these blanks and could use them for improper purposes. What do you do? You identify with him, of course! You say, "I never thought of that, and I can understand your quandary." At this point, because you have helped him by understanding his position, quite often he will do the job anyway. If not, you can leave to find another printer who will do the job.

Another example is a situation where you are questioned as to the authenticity of the birth certificate by someone like a motor vehicle department bureaucrat. Don't get mad, panic, or run to the door! Be polite, and suggest that you will contact the hospital that issued your original birth certificate or the Bureau of Vital Statistics from which you received the copy and find out why they issued such a questionable copy. Thank the person for calling the errors to your attention, pick up the document, and leave. In this way you eliminated any suspicions the bureaucrat had about you or the document itself. How many people are nice to motor

vehicle employees anyway? You probably made that
person's day. Then try again at another time and location to get what you need. Remember, if you learn to
capitalize on a person's psychological need to trust, and
his desire to know that what he is doing is right, you
will invariably succeed in achieving your end result.

The Infant Death Method (Long-Term)

The infant death method of obtaining a new identity
is used by the assassin in Frederick Forsythe's book *The
Day of the Jackal.* It involves taking on the identity of
someone who actually lived and died. Advantages are
numerous. By taking on the identity of someone who
died very young, no records, other than birth and death
certificates, exist. In other words, you become a person
with a clean slate. Second, a passport can be obtained
because when the certificate is checked out, it reveals an
actual existing person, and there is a record of the birth
certificate in the appropriate local agency office. Third,
it is the most complete, long-term method of altering
one's identity.

The basic concept is simple. It involves finding someone born at approximately the same time as you who
had the misfortune of dying young enough so that no
record exists as far as school, driver's license, credit
cards, or the like. You then apply for a certified copy of
the birth certificate and build a totally new identity
on the information it contains. In theory it is simple,
but total preparation is, as usual, the key.

The Approach

First, you must find the person you wish to become.
Be honest about how old you are and how old you look,
and note approximately what year someone would have
had to have been born to be nearly your age. Then you

ORIGINAL FILED

JUN 14 1982

COUNTY CLERK

CERTIFIED COPY

BY_____
                    CLERK

	Initials	Date
Prepared By		
Approved By		

RECEIVED

MAY 10 1982

BEVERLY HILLS MUNICIPAL COURT
9355 Burton Way
Beverly Hills, California 90210

Examples of Certification Stamps

must go about the task of finding the decedent. Some
manuals suggest that you actually search through grave-
yards to find the name that is to become your new identity. A more efficient method is to go to any research
library and review old newspaper obituary columns, usually found on microfiche or microfilm, for the name of
a child who died at, for example, four years of age, and
who was born at about the time you require. Any city,
county, or state will do at this stage. It is a good idea
to find more than one that fits the basic criteria as you
will be ordering each decedent's death certificate to find
out where the child was born, the county and state
where the death occurred, and whether the counties of
birth and death cross reference their records. You will
be looking for counties that do not cross reference, as
will be explained.

Where the Child Was Born

Almost all death certificates show where that person
was born. Anyone can order a death certificate over the
telephone or in person from the applicable jurisdiction's
Bureau of Vital Statistics, Hall of Records or the like.
Every county has its own records and its own rules
for obtaining them. It is up to you to learn the rules for
the jurisdictions in which you are interested. Remember, if an area is restrictive in its policy, you can always
use a cover or pretext for obtaining the death certificate
as will be explained in a later portion of this chapter.

Was the Child Born in Another County or State?

The ideal situation is to find a child who was born in
one state and died in another. If this ideal situation is
not available, being born in one county and dying in another will suffice. The younger the child, the less the
chance that he was born in one place and died in an-

other. This fact sometimes necessitates taking on the identity of a somewhat older child who might have lived long enough to move to another area with his parents, but remember, the younger the better. Try to combine both factors, the age of the child and the movement across county or state lines to your best advantage.

Does that County Cross Reference Birth and Death Records?

The reason we are interested in a young child who was born in one area and died in another is to avoid exposure of your assumption of that deceased person's identity. Many cities and counties cross reference their birth and death records. This means that in the birth certificate office, a notation will be made that that particular person died. Thus, if you were to assume that identity, there would always be irrefutable evidence in the birth certificate office that you were in fact "dead." By utilizing a name from an area where there is no cross referencing, your assumption of that person's identity will not be discovered if for some reason someone starts searching for you in the birth record offices. All they will find is a valid birth certificate, and no evidence that the person is not alive.

For example, to apply for a valid U.S. passport, it is generally necessary to provide a birth certificate. The passport offices then check the county records to confirm the validity of the birth certificate. If, upon checking under your assumed name, the clerk finds a notation that this person is indeed dead, you will be finding federal agents at your door. However, if this person did not come from an area where cross referencing exists, the clerk will find only a valid birth certificate, and your passport request will be honored.

After finding a decedent that was born and died in

different counties, you must then check to see if the two counties cross reference birth and death certificates. It should be obvious that the closer the towns, cities and/or counties are in proximity, the better the likelihood that cross referencing will exist. However, if you pick a death record in Las Vegas for a child who was born in Tampa, you can assume that you will be safe in taking on that new identity. To the best of my knowledge, no states, at the time of this writing, cross reference, nor does the federal government. It takes only a simple telephone call to the areas in question to develop the information on cross referencing. This one basic fact cannot be stressed enough. *The cross-referencing issue is imperative* and must be fully checked out before beginning the long-term identity assumption procedure.

Applying for the New Birth Certificate

Some counties' policies regarding the delivery of certified copies of birth certificates are not as defensive as others. As usual, it is advisable to check out these things before actually making the request so that nothing can take you by surprise. You should call the particular office in question and find out exactly what the procedure is and only then make your application. Normally, a request form will be involved, so be prepared to substantiate your identity with a business card, or some other form of identification so that your request will be honored without question. A general rule to follow is that the more rural the area, the more relaxed the policy.

There are unlimited reasons for requesting certified copies of birth certificates and once again, imagination is the key. A family member might be requesting the copy for an out-of-state sibling or for the local geneologist who is researching the family tree; an insurance in-

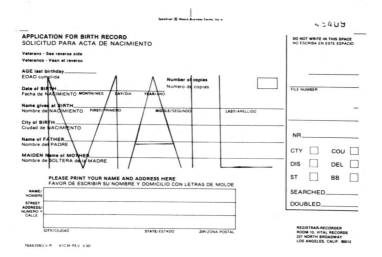

Application for Birth Record

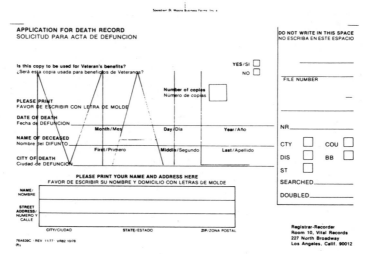

Application for Death Record

vestigator may be working on a fraud case; an attorney may be handling the disposition of a client's estate and needs substantiation of a beneficiary's existence; a county health examiner may be researching files; a priest may be doing a favor for an out-of-state parishioner (people never question priests). All one has to do is capitalize on the psychological need to trust and the inherent need to feel that what we are doing is right. If this is accomplished, the person with whom you are doing business will be more than happy to help. And always remember that it never hurts to smile.

Conclusion

Once one has obtained a birth certificate by either the counterfeit-forgery or infant death method, obtaining other types of identification is comically simple. Most important, don't be afraid to fail in your attempts to obtain your documentation. As long as you fail "smart," you will actually be gaining valuable experience. By failing smart I simply mean that you have done the very best job of preparation and presentation possible, but that for some reason, some uncontrollable, outside variable, your request has been denied. This is not truly failing, and it is important that you forget about the fact that you did not get the document, and extract the valuable lesson learned. Try to think about why your request was refused. How would you handle it differently next time? Was there some flaw in your technique? After analyzing all the facts, you will then be able to repackage yourself, and make another request at another time. Patience is a virtue here, and it will indeed pay off.

3. DRIVERS' LICENSES

Obtaining a driver's license and/or state I.D. card is perhaps the easiest step in obtaining good alternative identification. As discussed in Chapter 1 , the driver's license is utilized throughout the United States in a way that was never intended. This document entitles the bearer to operate a motor vehicle, not only in the issuing state, but in any other as well. It originally, and to this day, has no other legal purpose. Yet, the next time you attempt to cash a check, see how successful you are without a valid state driver's license.

Each state's qualifications and application requirements, as well as actual licenses, differ. In more rural states, simply applying guarantees a license. Why then is it nationally accepted as proof of identity? While more Big Brother oriented legislatures have suggested a national identity card, to date, the driver's license is the only uniform document almost everyone in our country possesses, and for the few who do not, states often provide I.D. cards that look like a driver's license. There seems to be a national, blind faith in the validity of the information on the driver's license. It is not yours to question why, only to accept and understand this phenomenon, and use it to your best and most profitable advantage.

Applying for the Driver's License

California is as restrictive as any state in its driver's license issuance policy, yet all one has to do is drive through the state and see the hordes of illegal aliens driving with valid drivers' licenses to realize how easy it is to obtain the document. California's policy requires only a minimum level proof of identity in order to qualify to take a driving test.

The most common identity qualifier is the birth certificate. As you will recall, we called this the cornerstone of the new identity in Chapter 2. Therefore, developing birth certificate information and presenting it when applying for a driver's license is foolproof and insures that you will be considered acceptable. But, it is not the only way to qualify.

Most states will also accept other forms of identity qualifiers. One document commonly accepted is the baptismal certificate. This document is filled in by a priest at the baptism of a young child. Fortunately for you, the beautiful certificate, complete with scrollwork, fancy lettering, and expensive-looking folder can be purchased by any citizen at religious supply stores. It can then be filled in and aged if necessary in the same way as the birth certificate.

I have often asked myself why state agencies place so much faith in the baptismal certificate. I was under the impression that the separation of church and state was something set forth in the Constitution. What I failed to realize is that government bureaucrats may be many things, but they are, at least on Sunday, generally religious human beings. When presented with that beautiful baptismal certificate, adorned with the holy figure of Jesus, fancy lettering, and the signature of a priest, a small switch is flipped in the brain, which automatically,

PRINT IN INK — ESCRIBA EN LETRA DE MOLDE EN TINTA

READ THE WARNING AND STATEMENT PRIOR TO SIGNING

LEA LA ADVERTENCIA Y DECLARACIÓN ANTES DE FIRMAR

1 Optional (Opcional) — Mr./Sr. ☐ Mrs./Sra. ☐ Miss/Srta. ☐ Ms ☐
Name - Nombre (first - primer) (middle - segundo) (last - apellido)

I am a citizen of the United States and will be at least 18 years of age at the time of the next election. I am not imprisoned or on parole for the conviction of a felony. I certify under penalty of perjury that the information on this affidavit is true and correct.

Soy ciudadano de los Estados Unidos y tendré por lo menos 18 años de edad para la próxima elección. No estoy preso o bajo el régimen de libertad provisional por un crimen de un delito grave. Juro bajo pena de falso juramento que la información en esta Declaración Jurada es verdadera y correcta.

2 Residence - Residencia (No. - Núm., Street - Calle, Apt. No. - Núm. del Apt.)

City - Ciudad   Zip Code - Zona Postal

11 Signature - firma   Date - fecha

▲

3 If no street address, describe location of residence: (cross streets, section, township, range, etc.) Si la calle no tiene núm. describa la localidad:/Calles que atraviesan, etc.)

AVISO

WARNING

4 Mailing Address (if different) - Direccion Postal (si es diferente)

Perjury is punishable by imprisonment in State prison for two, three, or four years. § 126 Penal Code.

El juramento en falso es castigable con encarcelamiento en la prisión del estado por dos, tres, o cuatro años. § 126 Código Penal.

City - Ciudad   State - Estado   Zip Code - Zona Postal

12 Signature of person assisting (if any)
Firma, de la persona que le ayuda (si hay alguien)

5 Date of Birth - Fecha de nacimiento   8 Occupation - Profesión

▲

(mo - mes / day - dia / year - año)

13 PRIOR REGISTRATION PORTION:
SECCIÓN DE PREVIO EMPADRONAMIENTO:

6 Name of State in USA or Foreign Country of Birth
Estado de EE.UU. o país de nacimiento

If you are currently registered to vote fill in portion below. Si Ud. está empadronado actualmente para votar llene los espacios abajo.

9 Telephone (Optional)
Teléfono (Opcional)

Name — Nombre

7 Political Party - Partido Político
(check one) (Indique uno)

10 I prefer election materials in . Prefiero materiales electorales en:

Former Address - Direccion Anterior

☐ American Independent Party
☐ Democratic Party
☐ Libertarian Party
☐ Peace and Freedom Party
☐ Republican Party
☐ Decline to state—Se niega a declarar
☐ Other—Otro _____

(Check one) (Indique uno)
☐ English
☐ Español

City - Ciudad   County - Condado   State - Estado

Political Party - Partido Político

OFFICE USE   ZJ 625920

STATE OF — ESTADO DE CALIFORNIA
COUNTY OF - CONDADO DE.
LOS ANGELES

AFFIDAVIT OF REGISTRATION —
DECLARACIÓN JURADA
DE EMPADRONAMIENTO

Driver's License Application

due to years and years of socialization, says "valid."
Again, don't question this unusual quirk of human nature; merely use it in your favor by understanding that
it does indeed exist.

Because what is good identity in one state is good
identity in another, all states will accept a sister state's
driver's license as proof of identity. Therefore, if you
find that one state's driver's license issuance policies
are more flexible and easier to satisfy than those of
another state where you would eventually like to get a
license, obtain the license in the state with the easy
policies, then take that license to the desired state and
merely turn it in for a new one.

Once again, preparation, planning, and imagination
are the keys. Call ahead and find out what documents
your particular area requires as proof of identity and
age in order to qualify for a driver's license. If a baptismal certificate can be used instead of a birth certificate,
great. If they require both, fine, as long as you know
this in advance and don't drop yourself into a sticky
situation by not knowing the outcome of the situation
before going into it.

As a footnote, don't worry if the state in which you
ultimately apply for a license requires that a photograph
appear on it. Photographs are not cross referenced with
any names, so they cannot be linked to any previous
identity. Some states offer choices between a photograph or a thumbprint. If this situation does arise,
always take the photograph. In most states, although
they can request that you provide a thumbprint, it is
not legally a condition of your obtaining a license there.
Therefore, do not feel intimidated, and most importantly, do not feel that you will be raising any undue
suspicion, if the clerk requests a thumbprint, and you

refuse to provide one. If done with confidence, this will not cause the clerk to think twice.

Conclusion

In day-to-day transactions between human beings, it is the driver's license which is the most commonly used source of identification. Be it the clerk at the checkout stand or the cop stopping you for a speeding ticket, an official-looking, state-issued driver's license provides irrefutable proof that you are who you say you are. Therefore, to function on a day-to-day level, the driver's license is perhaps the most important document in your wallet. But no one carries a driver's license and a driver's license alone. Ask some of your friends if you may merely peruse their wallets for an idea of what they carry in them. You will find a wide assortment of things, but besides a driver's license, in almost every wallet you find photographs, membership cards, identity cards, credit cards, and the like. These are what we call ancillary documents, and these ancillary documents should never be forgotten. For this reason, they are the subject of the next chapter.

4. ANCILLARY DOCUMENTATION

It is human nature to want to carry certain special or important things with us at all times. Some things that we carry have special sentimental value, others are merely practical in the course of day-to-day living. But what makes them all important to the person who is going to function under a new identity is merely the fact that these things do exist and are carried by almost everyone. Imagine a father not carrying pictures of his children, or a husband not carrying a picture of his wife. Try to imagine a businessman not having a credit card in his wallet, or a business card with his name, address and phone number. How many people do you know who do not have some form of identification card in their wallet so that if they are injured, or if the wallet is lost, someone can be notified? The answer is obvious, and for this reason, your new wallet must contain similar documents.

In reality, these ancillary documents are merely padding or icing on the cake. To have a photograph of your dog is not going to take you as far as having a driver's license or an American Express card, but since you are trying to become a new and total human being, you must have the documentation of a total human being. A naked wallet is a dead giveaway that something is wrong.

There are two basic levels of ancillary documentation. The first level is the easy-to-obtain, throwaway types necessary to function with a new identity. The second level, including checks, credit cards, check cashing cards, and the like, takes slightly longer to obtain.

Level One

This first selection of ancillary documentation serves to add credibility and substantiation to the information presented on, for example, a new driver's license. In and of itself, any particular piece of ancillary documentation would probably be insufficient to convince someone that the possessor is in fact that person identified. But taken in a group, along with other more commonly accepted forms of identity validation, this icing allows the trust mechanisms to flip on. This level one documentation is easy to obtain, yet it is all one really needs to round out a general purpose identification change. Examples include, but are not limited to, the following:

Business cards: Any investigator will tell you that business cards are one of the most useful tools in establishing a new identity. They can be printed quickly, inexpensively, and almost anywhere. Americans in particular have an almost inherent faith in business cards. You can be a doctor, a lawyer, or an Indian chief, so long as your business card says you are.

Library Card: An easy-to-obtain document, this shows both the name and address of its holder. Having a library card almost insures that you are a stable, well-educated, trustworthy citizen. For some reason, we seem to believe that criminals don't read.

Return If Lost Card: Most wallets come with this one. What "real" person wouldn't want his wallet returned if misplaced?

Membership Cards: With a minimum donation, you can

become a member of almost any group and receive an attractive membership card for your wallet. Again, membership cards in groups, cards, and organizations tend to show stability.

Social Security Card: The law does not require a person to carry an original Social Security card. For a few dollars, many companies will send you an attractive-looking Social Security-type card with any name and number you have given them. Here is a good identity validator, that is easily manipulated.

Insurance Cards: Many of the insurance companies that advertise on television and radio will, with any of their promotional materials, send along a membership card with your name emblazoned on it. These promotional materials cost nothing, and the card that normally comes with them is credit card size and quality and looks very official. Having your name embossed upon one of these official-looking cards certainly will go a long way in helping to validate your new identity.

Medical Emergency Card: Most drug stores carry these cards as giveaways and can be easily filled out with any information you desire.

Photographs: Photographs add the air of credibility to any wallet. Having a picture of a mother, father, boyfriend, girlfriend, or family pet will suffice, and should be included, as photographs are one of the most common wallet stuffers available.

Personalized Wallet: The real perfectionist can appreciate this one! Who would carry a wallet with his name or initials printed on it if he was not that person? Additionally, I have found that monogrammed shirts and initial signet rings are quite impressive.

Level Two

While the foregoing ancillary documents are sufficient for day-to-day business, those planning to stick with a

Examples of Ancillary Identification

new identity for any length of time will probably want a good supply of level two documentation. Level two is the ultimate in ancillary documentation and will be dealt with in the following chapters.

It is very important to remember, however, that what is set forth here is only a small list of all possible examples. These are not hard and fast rules and are meant to be expanded upon as required. The only rule is that you should carry whatever a normal person at your assumed income, education, and status level would carry on his person.

5. SOCIAL SECURITY CARDS

Misconceptions abound regarding a Social Security card and number. Like a driver's license, its intended use was simple and direct. A Social Security number represented your private account to hold paid-in benefits for your old age. It was essentially a coerced savings program initiated by Franklin Delano Roosevelt and was heralded at the time as a product of enlightened social conscience. Today, the Social Security system is broke, benefits provide a subhuman existence, and when it is time for you and me to retire, there will not be enough people paying in to foot the bill. So much for enlightenment.

You have probably noticed that everyone wants your Social Security number these days. Schools, lenders, banks—everyone seems to want it. Why? Because it is an easy way for individuals and the government to identify and keep track of you. It is one number you are supposedly stuck with your whole life.

The law only requires you to have a Social Security number to work in the United States. It does not require you to put it on anything that will not produce revenue for your account, with a very few exceptions found in the Privacy Act of 1974. In a nutshell, this says that no federal, state, or local government agency may deny you any right, benefit, or privilege for refusing to provide your Social Security number, unless there is a law or regulation on the books adopted prior to 1975, that specifically authorizes the demand for the number.

However, as with most, if not all, laws, there are some exceptions to the exceptions, and you may want to check these out.

Perhaps you have noticed that most government and private forms nevertheless ask for your number. The only true purpose is so that they can simply identify and keep track of you. In this situation, I always advise making one up or not giving one to them at all. Obviously you must make the distinction based upon the circumstances you are in. If it appears that the document you are trying to get will be difficult enough to obtain without causing undue obstacles to arise, perhaps it would not be wise to risk engaging the wrath of the person reviewing your application by not providing the number. They are not following your mentality, and you must therefore follow theirs. So don't play games, just make one up. It will appear a lot less suspicious to the clerk. Remember, don't let your ego get in the way; you're playing a game to win. Should you decide to use the false number, relax. There are no reliable ways for private concerns to authenticate your number once they have it. In fact, there are millions of Americans who have more than one!

Use of Another Social Security Number

There are two basic ways to obtain valid Social Security cards and numbers. One is simply to adopt someone else's. The other is to personally, or through a surrogate, apply for a card and number under new identification.

If you intend to make up a number, you must realize the purpose of the digital sequence used by the Social Security Administration. The first three digits correspond to the state in which the card is applied for. These are the key digits, and for this reason a chart is included so that you can make sure that these digits on your false I.D. card match those of the state where you allegedly applied. Again, not all bureaucrats go through their business days in a fog, blindly stamping "OK" on all the documents that pass their desks. Some will actually check up on these things, if only to fill empty time before lunch. These are the kinds of things you must be prepared for. So, check the enclosed chart and use it accordingly.

Of much, much less importance, but still something to consider, is the middle set of two digits. This tells the approximate year of issue. An odd number, between 05 and 09, was probably issued before the late 1930s, and an even number from 10 on up was probably issued after that. About fifteen years ago, previously unused two-digit sequences of even numbers, between 02 and 08 began to be circulated.

The final set of four digits can be utilized without any worry, as this set is meaningless, determined by the particular sequence at the office you signed up at and is virtually unverifiable.

If you want a card with the number of your choice on it, there are firms who, for a small fee, will print a Social Security-type card with your chosen name and number. A company that I have often used in the past is:

Dynamic Press
256 South Robertson Blvd.
Beverly Hills, California 90211

This is one of the few trustworthy companies that puts out a good, consistent product. All you have to do is provide them with the name and number, a stamped, self-addressed envelope, and five dollars. They very quickly return a professional-looking card to you.

One can successfully work as an independent contractor, or for short periods of time, as an employee of any job with a false Social Security number. But, working for extended periods of time under a fictitious number can cause minor problems. When an employer makes out a payroll check, he pays a percentage of what you have earned to your Social Security fund. About 50 percent of the time, if Social Security is receiving funds for an account from two unrelated sources, they will write the employers and ask them to verify their records as to the number. If it happens at all, it will generally happen within sixty days of submission. Your employer will then check the number's accuracy with you. That appears to be about the worst that will happen.

If you intend to work at an establishment for any length of time, it is probably a better idea to establish a "real" number.

Applying for a New Social Security Number

Applying for a new Social Security card under a false identity is not as difficult as one would assume. In contrast to its utility, it is downright simple.

A few basic facts are important. Like the Department of Motor Vehicles, the local Social Security office is looking for a minimum level of proof that you are who you say you are, and that you were either born in the United States, or are here lawfully. As mentioned before, if the evidence you present looks good to the individual helping you, a card will be issued. Social Security does not perform a background check to confirm if the information is valid. The Social Security Administration, and its local offices, epitomize bureaucracy out of control. The system is insolvent and its offices are understaffed. It should be obvious that it is a system that can easily be manipulated.

DEPARTMENT OF HEALTH AND HUMAN SERVICES
SOCIAL SECURITY ADMINISTRATION

FORM APPROVED
OMB NO. 72-878002

FORM SS-5 – APPLICATION FOR A
SOCIAL SECURITY NUMBER CARD
(Original, Replacement or Correction)

MICROFILM REF. NO. (SSA USE ONLY)

Unless the requested information is provided, we may not be able to issue a Social Security Number (20 CFR 422.103(b))

INSTRUCTIONS
TO APPLICANT ▶ Before completing this form, please read the instructions on the opposite page. You can type or print, using pen with dark blue or black ink. Do not use pencil.

1 NAME TO BE SHOWN ON CARD — First / Middle / Last
FULL NAME AT BIRTH (IF OTHER THAN ABOVE) — First / Middle / Last
OTHER NAME(S) USED

2 MAILING ADDRESS (Street/Apt No. P.O. Box, Rural Route No.)
CITY / STATE / ZIP CODE

3 CITIZENSHIP (Check one only)
a U.S. citizen
b Legal alien allowed to work
c Legal alien not allowed to work
d Other (See instructions on Page 2)

4 SEX: Male / Female

5 RACE/ETHNIC DESCRIPTION (Check one only) (Voluntary)
a Asian, Asian American or Pacific Islander (includes persons of Chinese, Filipino, Japanese, Korean, Samoan, etc. ancestry or descent)
b Hispanic (includes persons of Chicano, Cuban, Mexican or Mexican-American, Puerto Rican, South or Central American, or other Spanish ancestry or descent)
c Negro or Black (not Hispanic)
d North American Indian or Alaskan Native
e White (not Hispanic)

6 DATE OF BIRTH — MONTH / DAY / YEAR
7 PRESENT AGE
8 PLACE OF BIRTH — CITY / STATE OR FOREIGN COUNTRY

9 MOTHER'S NAME AT HER BIRTH — First / Middle / Last (her maiden name)
FATHER'S NAME — First / Middle / Last

10 a. Have you or someone on your behalf applied for a social security number before? No / Don't Know / Yes
If you checked "yes", complete items b through c below otherwise go to item 11
b Enter social security number
c In what State did you apply? / What year?
d Enter the name shown on your most recent social security card
e If the birth date you used was different from the date shown in item 6, enter it here — MONTH / DAY / YEAR

11 TODAY'S DATE — MONTH / DAY / YEAR
12 Telephone number where we can reach you during the day — HOME / OTHER

WARNING: Deliberately providing false information on this application is punishable by a fine of $1,000 or one year in jail, or both.

13 YOUR SIGNATURE
14 YOUR RELATIONSHIP TO PERSON IN ITEM 1 — Self / Other (Specify)
WITNESS (Needed only if signed by mark "X") / WITNESS (Needed only if signed by mark "X")

DO NOT WRITE BELOW THIS LINE (FOR SSA USE ONLY)
SUPPORTING DOCUMENT- / SSN ASSIGNED OR VERIFIED / DTC / SSA RECEIPT DATE
EXPEDITE CASE
DUP ISSUED / SSN / NPN
DOC / NTC / CAN / BIC / SIGNATURE AND TITLE OF EMPLOYEE(S) REVIEWING EVIDENCE AND/OR CONDUCTING INTERVIEW.
TYPE(S) OF EVIDENCE SUBMITTED
MANDATORY IN PERSON INTERVIEW CONDUCTED / DATE / DATE
IDN / ITV / DCL

FORM SS-5 (2-81) PRIOR EDITIONS SHOULD BE DESTROYED

Application for Social Security Number

INDEX OF SOCIAL SECURITY
NUMBERS BY NUMBER

001–003 New Hampshire
004–007 Maine
008–009 Vermont
010–034 Massachusetts
035–039 Rhode Island
040–049 Connecticut
050–134 New York
135–158 New Jersey
159–211 Pennsylvania
212–220 Maryland
221–222 Delaware
223–231 Virginia
232–236 W. Virginia
237–246 N. Carolina
247–251 S. Carolina
252–260 Georgia
261–267 Florida
268–302 Ohio
303–317 Indiana
318–361 Illinois
362–386 Michigan
387–399 Wisconsin
400–407 Kentucky
408–415 Tennessee
416–424 Alabama
429–432 Arkansas
433–439 Louisiana
440–448 Oklahoma
449–467 Texas
468–477 Minnesota
475–485 Iowa
486–500 Missouri
501–502 N. Dakota

503-504	S. Dakota
505-508	Nebraska
509-515	Kansas
516-517	Montana
518-519	Idaho
520	Wyoming
521-524	Colorado
525&585	New Mexico
526-527	Arizona
528-529	Utah
530	Nevada
531-539	Washington
540-544	Oregon
545-573	California
574	Alaska
575-576	Hawaii
577-579	District of Columbia
425-428	
&587	Mississippi

The United States Citizen Method

As can be determined from the information sheet put out by the Social Security Administration for applying for an original number, there are different categories of identifying data you will need to bring with you when applying. Category (1) is for U.S. citizens "born in the United States." I believe the U.S. citizen category, category (1), is the easiest to apply for.

By utilizing the information in this book, it should now be obvious that anyone can prove he or she is a U.S. citizen even if he or she is not. So if in reality you were born in Alabama or Argentina, it shouldn't make any difference for the purpose of your application, because you are the true creator of your new identity.

Most citizens of this country apply for their cards

between the ages of fifteen and twenty. This is about the time most teens are seeking their first jobs and need a card for that purpose. If in fact you are over eighteen when you apply, you must do so in person. Those under the age of eighteen are permitted to apply through the mail. As can be seen from the sample form, a minimum of two identifying documents are needed, one from list "A" and one from list "B." Sounds like the menu in a Chinese restaurant.

Age appears to be the biggest obstacle in the application of the U.S. citizen method. If you are considerably older than the fifteen-to-twenty age bracket and are applying for a card supposedly for the first time, the clerk may be interested in knowing why. Of course now that you are fully aware that creativity and theatrics are key elements in making any of these programs work, you will be prepared with a plausible story should you be questioned. Perhaps you could tell about how your parents supported you while you were in school, which included two different grad schools, and only now are you in a situation where you need to get a number and a job. Or how about the trips you took around the world, working with volunteer Christian missionaries in Zambia, until you were overcome with the plague and forced to return home? This works well with the "reborn" Christian clerk, who has a neck full of religious relics hanging conspicuously from an imitation gold chain. Just go in there realizing that the older you are, the more questions you may be confronted with and the more convincing you will have to be. But there is no reason to be intimidated. You must play the game of human psychology, and by now you should be pretty good at it.

Age is important only when applying. After that, you have a card and a number and no further age reference is made, not on the card, nor with the Social Security Administration. There are no checkups to worry about. In other words, if you are actually thirty-five years old, and your application lists you as twenty, no private party will have access to the file, nor will the Social Security Administration have reason to think that you are not the age listed on the application. They just don't have the time or money to worry about one out of the more than 200 million cards issued.

If you are applying as under eighteen, it is advisable to take the Social Security people up on their offer for applying through the mail. You must again play the menu game with regard to identifying documents, but you will have the obvious advantage of applying with the ultimate degree of anonymity. You can start by preparing a birth or baptismal certificate establishing your age as seventeen, for example. These documents will be duplicates of the ones you had made up pursuant to the instructions earlier in the book. If these documents have dates of birth on them, you will want to once again go to a printer and have the data removed unless it already corresponds to your age game plan. Do the same with some documents set out in the "B" list. Most printers would not think twice about reproducing school report cards, school I.D. cards, hospital or doctor's records, Boy or Girl Scout I.D. cards, or most of these other innocuous "B" list documents. Fill out the supporting documentation cards with information that conforms to that on your birth certificate or baptismal certificate. Then, write a letter on notebook paper, like a teenager would use, and simply explain that your family said you had to get a part-time job, and your employer asked if you have a Social Security card. Since you do not, the job is somewhat in jeopardy, and you want to get one as soon as possible. The return address you provide will of course be a mail drop or mail for-warding service in the jurisdictional area of the office in question. (See Chapter 6.)

An alternative method that normally works without a hitch is the surrogate method. With this method, you simply hire a teenager to apply in your new name at a Social Security office for your benefit. This avoids the delay of the mail, and since there are no photos on the cards, no one will be the wiser.

The Alien Method

To obtain a Social Security card as an alien, all one needs is an alien registration card (Green Card) or a U.S. Immigration form. Believe it or not, these documents are easier for a printer to reproduce than are birth certif-icates, and if you live in an area where immigrants are not a daily occurrence, he will be so accommodating to help one of the "tired and poor" of another land, that it's almost like asking him to print wedding invitations. Additionally, age does not matter with this technique as people often immigrate or obtain lawful work in the United States only at a later age.

Conclusion

When you are applying for a Social Security card, remember that the worst that can happen to you is that you will be turned down. There are thousands of local offices throughout the country, and therefore as many chances of getting your card. Ever consider going to Iowa or North Dakota or one of the other rural states in the Union, where requirements are as lax as they can be while still maintaining some semblance of offi-ciality? Some of my clients have done this. Whatever you decide the proper means will be, you have nothing to fear, and only a Social Security card to gain. As with applying for a driver's license, if you get turned down, be polite, collect your documents, and leave. No law has been broken, and you should not give any of the staff reason to think otherwise. If the office is large, don't be afraid to return at another time, to another window. Understanding human psychology and the inadequacies of this overgrown bureaucratic mess they call a system is the only real lesson to learn in obtaining a valid Social Security card.

6. MAIL DROPS AND ANSWERING SERVICES

Mail drops and answering services are a necessary and integral part of a new identity. This is particularly true if one is functioning under more than one identity at any given time. Mail drops and answering services create the image that a person has a stationary residential or business address, and that he has roots and ties in the community, when in fact he does not. The only time these services may not be necessary is if the new identity has been set up to start a new life entirely. In this case, one might want real addresses and community ties, such as a valid home address and phone number. This is only suggested if the identity has been created for very long-term usage.

Mail Drops

Aristotle Onassis was quoted by one of his many biographers as saying that even when he was young and poor, he maintained a good address. His reasoning, seemingly quite logical, was that no one was going to help him or give him the benefit of the doubt if he did not at least appear to be a person of substance.

The mail drop, or what is commonly referred to as a post office box, can make it difficult, if not impossible, for people to find where you really live or work. It can give others, including creditors, the impression that you live or work in a prestige location when in fact you do not. The mail drop can inexpensively give others a false sense of security that you and/or your business are rooted in the community. It creates the all-important sense of stability and permanence.

People use mail drops for countless reasons. I once knew an aspiring young social climber who wanted to tap the prestigious social contacts of New York's high society when in fact he was living hand-to-mouth. One of his ploys during this period was to have his mail delivered to a fashionable address in an exclusive area of New York. This address was, in fact, a mailing service that none of his well-heeled friends ever bothered to investigate. Today that person is easily recognizable as one of the nation's top designers and is on every socialite's guest list. Yet, had the beautiful people known of his original background and economic status, he would probably still be a manual laborer on the wrong side of the tracks.

Another friend, an aspiring young businessman, was determined to be a money manager and investment counselor to the creme de la creme of Beverly Hills, California. This was considered by his family to be quite a pipe dream considering this man could hardly afford a closet-sized office in the low rent end of town. Upon my recommendation, however, he located a mailing service in a prestigious building in Beverly Hills. This service even included a luxurious reception area, complete with a beautiful receptionist, offices, conference rooms, and secretaries all of which could be rented by the hour to give the impression that it was actually my friend's office. When the situation would arise that my friend could not convince a client to meet him at one of the finest restaurants in the city, he would rent his mail service conference room for a couple of hours, hire a secretary to come in and take notes of the meeting, and leave his newly found client stunned at the obvious success of his new financial advisor. Today, that same businessman has over thirty employees and is the financial counselor to the "who's who" of Beverly Hills and Hollywood.

Establishing the Mail Drop

The first step in successfully establishing a mail drop is to pick the best and most prestigious area of the city in which you intend to operate. This is particularly important when applying for credit or trying to convince would-be customers or clients to have faith in your services or product. Realize, of course, that the mail service does not have to be situated in a city or town where you actually reside. Many businesses that advertise their products in the backs of magazines, and have prestigious Beverly Hills or New York addresses, are actually located in small hamlets in the Midwest. They utilize mail drops and mail forwarding services to give potential customers the impression that the companies receiving their money are indeed secure and well established.

Most mail drops also have mail forwarding service, so that when your mail comes to the drop, it will be repackaged, restamped, then forwarded on to you. Your true identity and location is known only to the mail forwarding service. If you are interested in obtaining mail service in a town other than where you live, you merely need go to your local library and look through phone books for the cities in which you would like to establish your service. Mail drops are often listed under the headings of mailing services, secretarial services, mail forwarding services, or some derivative thereof.

Of paramount importance is the address of the ser-

Mail This Convenient Form Today

IF YOU PREFER TO SEND PAYMENT NOW FOR MORE
THAN ONE MONTH, JUST ENCLOSE THE APPROPRIATE AMOUNT.
(Send payment now for five months service and you
will receive one additional month free)

I WANT TO TAKE ADVANTAGE OF YOUR CONFIDENTIAL MAIL SERVICE. I AM ENCLOSING

$_ _ _ _ _ FOR _ _ _ _ MONTHS SERVICE (at $8.00 per month). I AM ENCLO-

SING AN ADDITIONAL $_ _ _ _ _ AS A DEPOSIT TO COVER THE COST OF STAMPS &

ENVELOPES USED IN FORWARDING MY MAIL TO ME.   TOTAL ENCLOSED: $_ _ _ _ _.

Name(s) in which mail will arrive_ _

Name and address to which you want your mail forwarded:

Name_ _ _ _ _ _ _ _ _ _ _ _ _ _ _ _ _ _ _

Street_ _ _ _ _ _ _ _ _ _ _ _ _ _ _ _ _

City_ _ _ _ _ _ _ State_ _ _ Zip_ _

Application for Mailing Address

vice. We have all seen ads for products which tell us to send our money to a post office in some particular city. Personally, I always hesitate to send money to these operations, as the mere fact that they are using a post office box makes me feel that they are shady.

Although I know in my mind that many companies use post office boxes to receive their mail in a convenient manner, my gut-level feeling, developed through years of experience, tells me that if they are receiving mail at a post office box, they must not be anything more than a business in someone's spare bedroom, and that if I send my money to them, I will probably never see it or the product, or maybe even the company advertisement again. For this reason, your mail drop should have a street address. For example, 351 Madison Avenue, Beverly Hills, California, sounds much more "real" than Post Office Box 8181, Beverly Hills, California. The former address could for all intents and purposes be an actual business address in the eyes of your potential customer or credit grantor. However, if you were to tell your credit grantor that your home address was Post Office Box 8181, your application would be promptly rejected.

There are many services that have these so-called normal street addresses, particularly in larger cities. If, however, you can only find a location that has box number designations, simply give your address as the address of the service, and list the box number as your suite number. For example, if your mailing service is at 351 Madison Avenue, Beverly Hills, California, but the owner requires that you put box number "201" on your mail, list your address as 351 Madison Avenue, Suite 201, Beverly Hills, California. The mail will arrive at your box just the same, and your address will look much more prestigious and solid. For your home address, put apartment 201 or unit 201.

Of course, one of the main reasons for using a mail drop is security and anonymity. For this reason, the more mailing services you can place between the person sending you the mail and your real location the better. By using the mail forwarding service mentioned above, you can have a mailing address in New York, which forwards your mail to a mailing address in Dallas, which forwards your mail to a mailing address in Las Vegas, which finally delivers the mail to your house in Chicago. Anyone trying to follow this circuitous path would have to be willing to spend enormous amounts of time and money to attempt to locate and pay off each service for the next forwarding address. Only once have I encountered a mailing service that was successfully paid off for my forwarding address, and I can assure you that they were dealt with in my own way, severely.

For the truly security conscious, the final resting place for your mail should be at a mailing service where you can go in and pick up whatever is in your box. Do not have them forward it to your true home or business address, for obvious reasons. Additionally, try to find a service that is open twenty-four hours a day. You can then pick up your mail at various hours of the day or night to ensure that you are not being followed or watched. I hope you realize that what I am preaching here is not paranoia, but only precaution. And, as one of my associates is so fond of saying, just because your friends tell you that you are paranoid doesn't mean that there aren't people out to get you! The bottom line is, the less human contact, the better. So if you can find a service that will serve as the final receptacle for your mail, one that is without a receptionist or that is large enough so that a receptionist cannot associate your face with your name, use it.

You should be wary of unanticipated, odd-shaped, or odd-colored packages mailed to you. These may be devices used by someone who is trying to identify you— you would be easy to spot walking out of the building with this unusual package. Once I went into one of my mailing services and was advised that they were holding a very large package for me in the back. They brought the package out, and I found that it was four feet long, yellow in color, and cylindrical in shape. What struck me first was that it was extremely lightweight, and when I shook it, there was absolutely no noise from the inside of the package. It was only then that I realized that there was no address, and only my name was on the cylinder. I asked the clerk how the mailman had delivered the package, and she replied that no mailman had delivered it, but that a "strange young woman" had dropped it off, saying that it was for me. I immediately, and quite carefully I might add, opened the package, only to find it absolutely empty. It was only six weeks later that I learned that this strange woman was actually trying to kill me and had been waiting across the street from the mailing service for me to walk out with the bright, yellow cylinder so that she could identify who I was and move in for the kill. Fortunately, the tables were turned on her, and she is now resting comfortably, as I understand it, in a state mental hospital. What I am saying is that if you are the recipient of an unusual package, let your curiosity get the better of you. The old saying about curiosity and the cat does not apply here. Carefully check out things that don't appear right. Do not take them at face value.

The requirements for establishing a mail drop differ

from business to business, but they are all quite simple. Most can be set up by mail or over the telephone and merely require a deposit and cursory application. Don't worry about the information you put on the application, as they are never checked out beforehand. These are businessmen trying to make money, not federal agents. Just make sure that you pay your bills in a timely manner, and you'll never have any problem.

Finally, most services will allow you to receive mail in more than one name, for example, a business name and an individual name. If this aspect is important to you, it should be researched in advance and taken advantage of.

Answering Services

Answering services go hand-in-hand with mail drops, and in fact, most mail drop companies also function as answering services as well. If you are telling someone that you are living or working in a fashionable part of town, it is important that the prefix of your telephone number be a prefix for that same part of town.

The best services will answer in your personal or business name. Others will answer with the last four digits of the business phone, such as "0475." You should avoid those that answer "telephone answering service" or "telephone secretary." It is not that these latter organizations are less efficient than the former, but it merely sounds a lot less impressive than a service that answers with your own name, or the last four digits of the phone number. Remember, you are trying to impress and intimidate people, while at the same time convince them of your stability and standing in the community. Simply place yourself in the shoes of that person who is calling you, and determine what would impress you. Good research before putting your money down will ensure that

you, as well as the people calling you, are happy with your telephone answering service. You should sample all of the answering services for professionalism, consistency, and quality. Remember, your influential business contacts and friends do not want to be put on hold or be verbally assaulted by a crabby operator.

Answering services, like mail drops, can normally be set up over the telephone or by mail. Most require an application similar to that of mail drops. For a truly professional setup, look in the *Wall Street Journal* for Telex and "800" numbers you can rent on a co-op basis with other subscribers.

These services will run you only about $25 per month and allow you to enjoy the ultimate in prestige. Few services are available even to the wealthy which carry the impact that an apparently private Telex and "800" number have. While the average lay person knows these services exist, few, if any, have ever heard of anyone less than the chairman of the board having access to them.

From a security standpoint, answering services, like mail drops, can further insulate you from the personal problems of both wanted and unwanted callers. It is up to you to call in for your messages on a regular basis, while you rest assured that your real phone number will only be given out to those few important people whom you feel need it.

Conclusion

With a prestigious mailing address and a professional answering service, you are proving to others that you are the success that you say you are. However, if for some reason, you are trying to convince others that you are merely middle-class, or lower, it is certainly easy to establish the same setup in a less than prestigious part of town. Your circumstances dictate exactly how the program is to read. On a daily basis, you mail information to addresses that are only mail drops. You call telephone numbers that are only answering services. People believe these outward manifestations because they are given no reason to doubt them. And that's just how we want it.

7. FALSE BUSINESS ENTITIES

Establishment of a false business entity is easily accomplished and can be done for any number of reasons. People are generally impressed by what appears to be a legitimate and successful partnership or corporation. It can smooth the road for obtaining credit, getting loans, and as will be seen in the next chapter, setting up bank accounts. Almost any transaction can be more easily accomplished by a business entity as it connotes a high degree of solvency and stability in most people's minds. For obvious reasons, a man who has his own business is considered a success in America. A false I.D. is not necessary for setting up a business entity, but as always, it can be helpful.

Business entities can be set up by two methods, depending on one's purpose. They are: the quasi-legal method and the fictitious method.

Quasi-Legal Method

The quasi-legal method is used to legitimately establish the business entity, for example, a partnership, limited partnership or corporation, by making the required filings with the various governmental authorities. In this instance, all of the proper government formalities are complied with, but for the fact that valid information is not given. For example, the owners of the business are listed, but the names given are the names you have adopted as alternative identification. The address of the business is a mail drop. The telephone number is an answering service. If a corporation, the agent for service of process, required in most states to be on file with the Secretary of State, is again a fictitious person, whose identity is set forth, but who, in reality, does not exist. (In this situation, if the corporation is sued, the process server will find an almost impossible task in attempting to locate, as is required by law, the non-existent agent for service of process.)

In effect then, what you have under the quasi-legal method is documentation that can be checked up on as being on file as required by law. Unfortunately for the person doing the checking, any further attempt to investigate the owners of this seemingly legal business will only result in failure.

Fictitious Method

The fictitious establishment of a business entity involves filling out the necessary government applications and forms, but never recording them with the governmental authorities. Essentially you make the documents look official for the purposes of establishing bank accounts and conducting business, when in fact they are not.

Establishing a Corporation

Despite all of the negative propaganda written about it, people do believe in the business corporation. The average person on the street will tell you that a corporation connotes credibility and stability much more than a mere individual doing business in his own name. People are impressed by corporations. Even the word *corporation* sounds impressive, imposing, and intimidating. It sounds big, and big sounds powerful. To the average lay person, a corporation has lots of money and with lots of money comes lots of power and influence.

What most people do not realize is that by design a corporation insulates the wealthy individual who owns it from personal liability. What this means in reality is that there is less chance of recouping an investment from a corporation than from an individual. Many times, the owner of a corporation will bleed the corporate bank accounts dry for his own benefit. When the investors attempt to sue, they run into what is known as the "corporate veil," which generally shields the owner from liability. The theory in the law is that if a corporation does something wrong, you cannot sue the owner, as the corporation itself stands in the eyes of the law as a legal "person." Even smart doctors, lawyers, and bankers, who should know that the people behind impressive-sounding corporations are often protecting themselves from ultimate liability, are easily impressed when doing business with a corporation. This obviously can and should be used to your advantage. Remember, all of us have certain psychological keys or "hot buttons" which can be manipulated by smart people.

As mentioned previously, businesses, like corporations, can be set up in two ways, depending on one's purposes. Both work equally well and the utilization of one over the other is a matter of personal preference.

Quasi-Legal Corporation

Attorneys charge hundreds of dollars to perform the comically simple task of incorporating a business. Each state differs slightly, but only slightly, in the requirements for setting up a corporation, so check with the Secretary of State in your particular state capitol for the requirements. Many states will even send you the blank forms to fill out. If these are not available, most stationery stores have preprinted legal forms which can be filled out and readily utilized. Basically, all that is generally required is the filing with the secretary of state of a document known as the Articles of Incorporation, along with a nominal filing fee. The Articles of Incorporation requests only a minimal amount of information and can easily be manipulated to your advantage. As mentioned above, you can merely fill out the form in a fictitious name, with mailing addresses, pay the fee, and have the document recorded. The secretary of state will then return a copy of your Articles to you, complete with an official stamp, which confirms that you are a valid business corporation in that particular state.

In order for your corporation to look and feel official and most impressive, you should have a complete corporate minute book with a corporate name embossed on it, corporate bylaws, and a corporate seal with stock certificates. This is easily obtainable and can be purchased through any legal supply house. To get the name of a legal supply house in your area, merely check in the phone book or go to a lawyer's office and ask him where he gets his legal supplies.

An even easier method is to utilize the services of one of the many incorporating companies that have popped up around the country in the past few years. For a small fee over and above the filing fee, these companies will prepare the necessary documents, file them, and return the approved Articles along with the corporate minute book to you. All you have to do is supply the information to them. These companies are often found in the yellow pages under the heading "incorporating services" and many even advertise in the classified ads of the Sunday newspapers under the "legal services" heading.

ARTICLES OF INCORPORATION

OF

Filed with Secretary of State

_____, 19___

ARTICLE I

The name of this corporation is _____

ARTICLE II

The purpose of this corporation is to engage in any lawful act or activity for which a corporation may be organized under the **General Corporation** Law of California other than the banking business, the trust company business or the practice of a profession permitted to **be** incorporated by the California Corporations Code.

ARTICLE III

The name and address in the State of California of this corporation's initial agent for service of process is:_____

_____

ARTICLE IV

The corporation is authorized to issue only one class of shares of stock; and the total number of shares which this corporation is **authorized**

to issue is _____.

DATED: _____

_____

(Signature(s) of Incorporator/Director(s))

I (we) hereby declare that I (we) am (are) the person(s) who executed the foregoing Article of Incorporation, which execution is my (our) **act** and deed.

NOTES: 1. If this is to be a close corporation:
   a. The word "incorporated", "corporation", or "limited", or an abbreviation of one of such words must appear in the name.
   b. An Article V must be typed in above and should say: "This corporation is a close corporation. All of the corporation's issued shares of **stock** shall be held of record by not more than ten (10) persons."
2. If it is desired (it is not necessary) to name the directors in the articles:
   a. An Article V or VI must be typed in above and should say "The names and addresses of the initial directors are as follows: _____ " Each director so named must also sign and acknowledge the articles.
3. If directors are not named in the articles, the incorporator's name and address should be typed below his signature.

WOLCOTTS FORM 436. REV. 1-77 ARTICLES OF INCORPORATION. SHORT FORM

Filing the Articles of Incorporation

Fictitious Corporation

As was seen above, all that is generally required to incorporate is the filing of the Articles with the secretary of state, along with a small filing fee. We also learned that in order to look official, various documents such as bylaws and stock certificates should be obtained and placed in an attractive, official-looking corporate minute book. The only difference between the quasi-legal and the fictitious corporation method is that in the latter, recordation of the Articles never actually occurs. Additionally, the information filled out on the bylaws, stock certificates, etcetera, is false.

In a nutshell, what this method requires is the creation of documents that appear as though they have been filed. This can be accomplished in a number of ways.

The same techniques used to prepare new birth certificates can be implemented here. The most useful tools are rubber stamps, rub-on appliques, and embossing stamps, all of which can be obtained from almost any print shop. Invariably, documents such as the Articles of Incorporation, when filed with the secretary of state, are simply stamped with some kind of stamping device. For example, in one state, the stamp which goes in the upper right-hand corner of the Articles reads as follows:

FILED with the Secretary of State.
March 18, 1983
By _____
                    Clerk

After finding out exactly what type of stamp is used in your state, you can have it copied by your local print shop, prepare your own documents, and, without ever having to file, stamp them so that they are "official." If you need to look at a sample from your local area, merely consult a lawyer under a pretext, ask a friend who has a friend who has a corporation, or file an actual corporate document yourself so that you can receive a copy of the stamped Articles. This can give you a guide to follow for further implementation. In the alternative, you can create a corporation from a state such as Montana or Idaho, as most people would not have any reason to ever come in contact with corporate documents from these states and would have no way of telling whether your documents, as stamped, were in fact proper. Again, it is imperative to have a good selection of rubber stamps, changeable character rubber stamps, and embossing seals so that official-looking documents can be created in the privacy of your own home.

Remember, these documents are going to be presented to human beings for review. Human beings, by nature, do not carefully scrutinize and are rarely familiar enough with the real thing to say whether or not those you have are proper. Additionally, if you look and play the part, your intimidation factor will make people hesitant to question you. This obviously works in your favor. Even if your Articles of Incorporation are not stamped correctly and you are trying to open a business bank account, both the ignorance on the part of the banker as to the correct character of such documents and your intimidation factor will probably assure success. If it looks official, it will do the job. After all, even if your banker has seen hundreds of these documents before, he would have no way of knowing if, in the past week or so, the Secretary of State's validating stamp had been changed. Even in the most bureaucratic and red tape-laden states, some changes do occur!

A true perfectionist can go one step further. Like the birth certificate, anything can be altered and reproduced from an original. I know one person who filed the Articles of Incorporation in 1957, obtaining a stamped copy from the secretary of state who readily accepted this proper document. From this one document, my friend has reproduced, and in effect created out of thin air, hundreds of corporations, merely by getting a good-quality photocopy of the Articles, removing the date stamped by the secretary of state, reapplying his own date and new name, rerunning the copy as corrected, and stamping it "Certified." He has come up with beautiful copies that have been utilized in many, many countries throughout the world to obtain hundreds of thousands of dollars for his scheming ways. Unfortunately, this man has lost most of this vast fortune through bad business investments and an excessive gambling habit.

Business Licenses

Obtaining a local business license and filing a Fictitious Name Statement to operate under an assumed name such as "Acme Widgets" is simple. Most cities require every business established within its borders to obtain a business license for tax purposes. Additionally, if one is to do business in a name other than one's own, a document known as a Fictitious Name Statement is often required. This document, which becomes part of the public record, indicates that Mr. John Smith is doing business as "Acme Widgets." Because of this filing requirement, anyone wanting to locate the actual owner of the business known as "Acme Widgets" merely has to review the Fictitious Name Rolls, and could thereby easily locate Mr. Smith as the owner. It might even require Mr. Smith to give his residential address as part

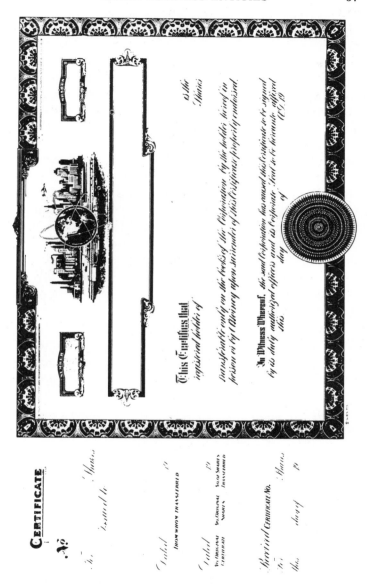

Corporation Stock Certificate

of the filing requirements! This public record is often utilized by process servers when trying to serve a business owner who cannot be readily identified or located.

Each state differs slightly in its requirements and procedures for the business license and Fictitious Name Statement, also known as the DBA (DBA stands for *doing business as*). However, for you the bottom line is the same. These documents can be utilized to your advantage by filling them out with fictitious information. By doing this, you have the advantage of further establishing your bona fide status in the community as an upstanding, tax-paying citizen who files the required forms as mandated by the municipality. In reality, you have a total business front, and for this reason, it is almost impossible for that municipality or its agents to control or inhibit your true activities.

As an additional bonus, which I am sure many of the sharper readers of this book have already thought of, it is very, very difficult for the tax collector to collect taxes from a business entity that does not in fact exist! Many people merely shut down operations immediately prior to tax time only to resurface some months later under a different, but equally fictitious, business structure. Are you doing anything wrong, or merely protecting your own best interests? This is for you to decide. I've only given you some food for thought, and I hope it was easy to digest.

Conclusion

Because each state is sovereign unto itself and differs in the exact documents required to conduct business, preparation, preparation, preparation is the key. The proper application of the basic procedures outlined in this chapter, coupled with some minor investigation as to the state's requirements, will ensure success. You

05096

PRINTED BY THE STANDARD REGISTER COMPANY, U.S.A. ZIPSET ®

LOS ANGELES COUNTY CLERK
CORPORATION UNIT, ROOM 106
111 N. HILL STREET
LOS ANGELES, CALIFORNIA 90012

REMINDER
1. Submit Original and 3 copies
2. Filing Fee $10.00.
3. Provide return Envelope, if mailed
4. Remove carbons before mailing

SEE REVERSE SIDE FOR INSTRUCTIONS

FICTITIOUS BUSINESS NAME STATEMENT

THE FOLLOWING PERSON(S) IS (ARE) DOING BUSINESS AS:

1. Fictitious Business Name(s)

2. Street Address, City & State of Principal place of Business in California | Zip Code

3. Full name of Registrant | (if corporation - show state of incorporation)

Residence Address | City | State | Zip Code

Full name of Registrant | (if corporation - show state of incorporation)

Residence Address | City | State | Zip Code

Full name of Registrant | (if corporation - show state of incorporation)

Residence Address | City | State | Zip Code

Full name of Registrant | (if corporation - show state of incorporation)

Residence Address | City | State | Zip Code

4. This business is conducted by ( ) an individual ( ) a general partnership ( ) a limited partnership (CHECK ONE
( ) an unincorporated association other than a partnership ( ) a corporation ( ) a business trust ONLY)

5.
Signed _____

Typed or Printed _____

If Registrant a corporation sign below:

Corporation Name _____

Signature & Title _____

This statement was filed with the County Clerk of Los Angeles County on date indicated by file stamp above

6. New fictitious business name statement ☐

7. Refile. Statement expires Dec. 31st. ☐

FILE NO. _____

CERTIFICATION
I hereby certify that the foregoing is a correct copy of the original on file in my office.

JOHN J. CORCORAN, County Clerk

By _____ Deputy

FILE NO. _____

76F 3860 F-29 (REV. 9/78)

FILE WITH COUNTY CLERK

Filing the Fictitious Business Name Statement

should obtain and carefully review all documents you will need to set up your business in the city of your choice. Do not, as so many have foolishly tried to do, present yourself at the filing window unprepared, and then stumble and stutter as you try to explain to the now suspicious clerk why your driver's license name and the name that you have just signed on your Fictitious Name Statement do not match. When you walk through the doors of that office, you should be so confident in your preparation that your pen could almost fill in the forms by itself. All you will have to do is stand by confidently smiling at the clerk who is so appreciative of the fact that finally, finally, one applicant has taken the time to read the instructions and complete the document correctly.

8. BANKING

While the image they portray is that of patron saints, banks can be your enemy as well as the government's friend. The laws are such that they can *and do* annually disclose all of your banking transactions to the I.R.S. If you deposit or withdraw $10,000 or more in one lump sum, banks automatically report it to the government, pursuant to legislative requirements. It is therefore quite wise and prudent to think of your bank as merely another arm of the federal government. But this is not to say that you have to bury your money in a coffee can in the backyard or stuff it under your mattress.

Acknowledging that the United States banking system is not necessarily your friend is the first step in successfully banking under an alternative I.D. The average bank employee is a stereotypical bureaucrat, not very smart, not very imaginative, and somewhat tunnel-visioned. Typically, he is underpaid, overfed, and constantly plagued by the monthly mortgage. Realizing the bureaucratic nature of banks and their employees makes them easy to take advantage of.

For example, a friend of mine has a successful retail electrical supply company that is now even more successful because he pays taxes only on approximately 50 percent of his revenue. Because most of his customers pay by check, he came to me to try to figure out

71

a way to clear these checks through a bank without creating records for the government. The solution was to have a percentage of his customers make their checks payable to a common name like "Acme, Inc." He then established a business banking account across town under this name with nonexistent owners. On a yearly basis, right after the banks report account activity to the government, he moves the funds, changes the name, and starts the process over again.

Another associate of mine, whose cash businesses net him far more than he would want to keep under his mattress, uses a similar technique. His banking is done under many false names and immediately after the bank's yearly government reporting, he moves the accounts and establishes them under new names.

By implementing the information contained in this chapter, you will find banking under fictitious business or personal identification easy and practical. You will also discover how to take advantage of the banks and not allow them to take advantage of you.

Establishing a Personal Account

Banks have fairly standardized procedures for establishing personal accounts. Because of this, utilization of false I.D. is simple. The banks ask for identification and you produce enough to convince the account representative, usually the lowest paid bank employee, that you are who you say you are. A driver's license is normal, but depending upon the bank, one of the many forms of ancillary documentation can successfully be used. A Social Security number is also required (although not by law) so provide them with a false one as discussed in the chapter on Social Security cards and numbers. Most banks will also ask you for your mother's maiden name. The purpose for this is merely to identify you if all other sources of identification fail. Of course, you do not want to use her real maiden name, but a fictitious one, which can easily be recalled if needed. It is interesting to note that the Social Security number you give them is only used for reporting purposes and is rarely, if ever, used as an identification source.

Unless you want to establish a personal relationship with the bank hierarchy, anonymity is the order of the day. Many banks will let you send most of the filled-in application material through the mail, and this is suggested, as the fewer personal contacts with any staff members, the better. Under this circumstance, you can merely tell them that you are picking up the application material for your boss or your invalid grandmother, and that the information will be returned via the mail. If it is required that a signature card be signed in person, pick a busy time on the busiest day of the week, such as Friday or payday when the bank is overrun with people, to go in and take care of these formalities. Typically, the account representative will just want to get you out of her hair, and you will get in and out of the bank in a matter of minutes.

If true anonymity is what you want, make sure the bank has one of the new automated teller machines. By using this mechanical wonder, you can do all of your bank transactions from outside the bank, after hours, and will never again have to establish any contact with bank personnel. Between check books, deposits by mail, and the automated teller, there should never be any reason to set foot inside the bank under any circumstances once the account is opened.

Banks typically report to the government in January on the preceding year's activities. So if you have funds that you do not want traced, movement of your account in January or February is a splendid idea.

Business Banking

Setting up a business account is preferable for the depositor who works with large amounts of money. This is due to the fact that most individuals do not have huge amounts of cash in personal accounts while businesses do. Again, playing upon human psychology is paramount. While it is certainly not improbable that an individual would come in to deposit or withdraw $15,000, it would raise more eyebrows than if it was done under the guise of a business entity. Another advantage of using the business account is that this type of account further insulates the individual from any connection with it. For this reason, banks are slightly more restrictive in the establishment of the business account.

The real difference between establishing a business versus personal account is simply that banks need some evidence that the business indeed exists. While the establishment of a personal account merely requires a driver's license or equivalent document, the business account typically requires city or state-issued documentation such as the business license, tax permit, Articles of Incorporation, etcetera. But, as you have already read, this type of documentation is easy to come by through either the quasi-legal or fictitious method. The important thing to remember is that banks badly want and need your money. Business accounts represent considerable available funds for bank usage on which they have to pay little in the way of interest. So, if you walk into one of the smaller banks with $10,000 to open a business account, bank personnel will do anything short of, but maybe even including, shining your shoes in order to get you to drop that money in their vault.

Choosing the Bank

Choosing the bank for a commercial account is the first step, particularly if you want anonymity. The larger, more well-known the bank, the more money it will take to impress bank officials. The rule of thumb is simply to be an average commercial account for that particular bank. If your opening account is too small, a big bank will make it difficult for you with too many formalities. If your opening account is too large, you might be its largest depositor and this kind of notoriety is something that you generally don't need. I have always preferred the smaller commercial banks for amounts up to $100,000. Their policies are traditionally more lax because they so aggressively seek business. The key is to use practical judgment. If the bank or its personnel don't seem right for you, there are many, many others to choose from.

If the conditions warrant it, you may certainly choose a bank for its name, address, board of directors, or any one of a number of reasons. Again, all I am trying to do is open your eyes. It is up to you to focus them on your target.

Opening the Account

Banks traditionally want two things to open a commercial account: Some form of evidence that the business is legally organized, and the signature of the authorized signatory on a bank signature card.

Evidence of the validity of your business varies from bank to bank and depends upon how badly they want or need your business. As mentioned above, a business license, Fictitious Name Statement, Articles of Incorporation, or business tax permit will immediately give you access to an account. It is up to you to determine

ACCOUNT AGREEMENT – ORGANIZATION
(CORPORATION, UNINCORPORATED ASSOCIATION, PARTNERSHIP, JOINT VENTURE)

ACCOUNT TITLE   ACCOUNT NUMBER

KIND OF ACCOUNT	NATURE OF ACCOUNT	
☐ CHECKING ACCOUNT, REGULAR	☐ CORPORATION	☐ PARTNERSHIP, GENERAL
☐ TIME DEPOSIT, OPEN ACCOUNT (BONUS PASSBOOK), MATURITY	☐ UNINCORPORATED ASSOCIATION	☐ PARTNERSHIP, LIMITED
☐ SAVINGS ACCOUNT, REGULAR	☐ CORPORATE FIDUCIARY	☐ JOINT VENTURE
☐ MOBILE MONEY ACCOUNT	☐ CONTROLLED, Subject to:	
☐		

This undersigned organization (corporation, unincorporated association, partnership, or joint venture as specified above) agrees with the CROCKER NATIONAL BANK as follows:

This account and all deposits therein shall be of the kind and nature indicated above, and subject to all applicable laws and to the Bank's present and future by-laws, rules, regulations, practices, and charges.

The Bank may honor, receive, certify, or pay all checks, drafts, orders, receipts, and other instruments drawn, accepted, or given by the undersigned for payment from the account or at the Bank when, if designated "Corporation", "Unincorporated Association", or "Corporate Fiduciary", signed by such persons as the directors of the corporation or the directors, officers, or trustees of the association may authorize and the secretary or other authorized person may certify to the Bank from time to time; and, if designated "Partnership" or "Joint Venture", signed by such persons as the undersigned may certify to the Bank from time to time.

The Bank may (a) accept for deposit or collection any check or other instrument payable to the organization, the undersigned, cash, or bearer, whether or not endorsed by written or stamped endorsement with or without designation or signature of the person making the endorsement, or cash any such check or instrument if endorsed in the same manner as is authorized for signing on the account; (b) at the organization's risk (1) mail or deliver statements and related items to the organization, (2) hold or otherwise dispose of them as requested by the undersigned, and (3) if "Will Call" is specified in any said signature certification, hold them until called for by any one authorized to sign on the account; (c) if given conflicting certifications or demands, either deposit the balance in court or withhold payment from the account pending the joint order or receipt of all parties or an appropriate court order determining those authorized to sign; and (d) without notice or demand apply or set off any balance in the account against any obligation of the organization to the Bank when due.

If the account is designated (a) "Savings", the undersigned warrants that it is entitled to maintain a savings account under Regulation Q of the Board of Governors of the Federal Reserve System and that the Bank may require 30 days' written notice of an intended withdrawal; (b) "Time Deposit, Open Account", funds are to remain on deposit until, and may not be withdrawn before, the above-stated maturity; (c) "Partnership" or Joint Venture", those signing below certify that they are all of the general partners or joint venturers thereof; if the organization is doing business under a fictitious name it warrants that it has title to and right to use the same and has complied with all requirements for using or doing business under that name and that the Bank may accept for deposit, collection, or encashment any instrument payable to or endorsed in that name; (d) "Controlled", the Bank may require appropriate additional authorization to pay monies from the account.

The "undersigned" means, as the case may be, the corporation, association, or any general partner or joint venturer signing below:

_____, 19____

```
..........................................
:          (SEAL)                        :
:                                        :
:                                        :
:                                        :
:                                        :
:                                        :
:                                        :
:      (If none, so state)               :
..........................................
```

CUSTOMER'S SIGNATURE

_____

_____

_____

_____

_____

05-3068(REV.2-60)

Application for a Business Banking Account

how you are going to provide these documents.

I remember the first time I tried to open a business account with a very small bank. I was naturally somewhat timid since this was the first time, and I was only eighteen years old. I mailed in all of the required documentation, including a fictitious business permit application which I had filled out, but never filed. Approximately two weeks later they returned the whole package of documents to me, asking that I come in, with these same documents, and fill out a signature card. At the time I remember being totally crestfallen as my plan had not worked. I had not done my homework; I did not realize that a signature card would be required and that I would have to go into the bank in order to prepare one. However, being persevering, I realized that something in that return package could be used to my benefit. This "something" was a letter prepared and signed by the bank manager. In the letter, he thanked me for applying to the bank for a business account. He went on further to state that it would be necessary for me to come into the bank to prepare a signature card, and that while I was there, he would like to shake my hand and get to know me a little bit better. The letter was signed with warm regards, and with that and the bank manager's signature, I realized I virtually had a key to the bank!

The next day I found out what time the manager was going to lunch. At that same hour I went into the bank and presented my documentation to the account representative along with the letter from "my old friend," the bank manager. This clerk, who saw a letter on bank letterhead, signed by the manager, was so immediately impressed and intimidated, that he did not even read the letter to see that I had never even met his boss! To him, the fact that I had this letter in my possession was evidence that I must be somebody. From that point, getting my account opened was easy. I presented the letter and, without any other form of identification, signed the signature card under my alternative identity and left the bank. Two weeks later, a beautiful book of 200 blank checks arrived at my mailing address, and I was never so happy and proud in my life. I had utilized psychology and intimidation to its practical end, that being the establishment of a viable business bank account under false identification. To this day the bank account still exists though I have never written a check in that checkbook. It stands on my bookcase like a trophy, and I will always cherish it as one.

Another interesting event occurred when I rented a limousine (before I bought my own) and had it parked in front of the bank where I wanted to open a fictitious business account. I got out of the limousine in plain sight of everyone and hurriedly entered the bank wearing a beautiful suit and carrying an expensive briefcase. My chauffeur opened the door of the car and then the bank. Upon approaching the manager, I gave him my false business card fervently hoping he didn't finger it too much as the ink was barely dry! I then nonchalantly tossed $10,000 in cash on his desk, told him I was rushing to catch a plane, and wanted a business account opened immediately for my company's executive expansion in his city. I also informed him that this was merely an opening deposit and more money would be going into the account on a weekly basis. Needless to say, this overstuffed bank manager practically had a coronary trying to accommodate me. I then offered to mail him anything he might need, which I never did, and had an account when I left. Had he troubled to call the long distance number on my card, he would have gotten my telephone service answering as the fictitious business. What I essentially did was intimidate the manager into doing precisely what I wanted. While one does not usually need to go to such extremes, the point should be well understood.

Conclusion

As usual, if one has set up a false I.D. or fictitious business, opening a bank account can be quite simple. But while it is easier, it is not imperative. Like establishing any other new I.D. in this book, all that is really necessary is a positive mental attitude that will allow you to fail and still try again.

I have failed on occasion while learning and so might you while assimilating the material in this book. But remember, if you present yourself correctly, the worst anyone will ever do is say no. Most will say yes.

9. CREDIT CARDS

Credit cards are really a product of the last two decades, yet it is hard to imagine getting along without them in modern society. With the prices of things today, you would need to carry a wallet two inches thick with money to pay for food and gasoline in cash. The credit card is the perfect tool for a consumer society as it allows people to buy now and pay later. A wonderful system until the bill comes!

Having credit cards can represent a kind of absurd respectability. People even look down on those who do not have them, as though they represent membership in some kind of exclusive club, instead of realizing that some people rationally choose to live debt-free. Nevertheless, credit cards are a necessary evil in today's society.

Obtaining credit is a game. You have to learn what the rules are if you want to play the game correctly and successfully. It is the credit company that makes the rules, and you can play successfully only if you follow the rules it creates. It expects you to measure up to its own notions of a good credit risk and if you do, it will let you in on the playing field. Therefore, it is important to realize that merely knowing the rules of the game is not the same as having the ability to play. As in any game, you must have a strategy, a plan of attack.

The real winner not only learns the rules, but also learns how to use them to his best advantage.

The first rule of the credit game is that credit availability is directly proportional to the general economic condition of the society in which it is granted. When the economy is bad and you need credit most, it is the hardest to get. When the economy is good and cash is readily available, credit is easiest to obtain. For this reason, the methods for obtaining credit discussed here should be used as a general outline only. For example, there is a standard and a short-term method of gaining credit discussed in this chapter. In a poor economy, the thirty-day short-term method requires more diligence on the applicant's part to succeed.

The Standard Approach

There is a point in everyone's life when he seeks credit for the first time. No one is born with credit unless he has wealthy parents, so most of us start at basically the same place—zero. Obtaining credit under a new I.D. is no more difficult for one person than it is for another. Everyone works up from zero.

The standard approach for obtaining credit must be understood before any quick, short-term method can be implemented. One has to understand the rules of the game before he can successfully play.

Like anything else, the first step is the hardest. Obtaining credit is a building-block procedure which resembles a pyramid. If one places the cornerstone properly, the rest of the structure falls easily into place. If you think of yourself not as a person with a fake I.D., but simply as a new person in town trying to get established, you will find it simple and even fun. As a new resident in town, where would you look for new credit? The answer is at the corner store. Therefore, as a person operating under a new identity, the corner store becomes your primary focus also.

Personally, I believe in starting at these lower-end stores for one simple reason. Should you try applying at a middle or upper-level store and get turned down, your credit report (which will be established as you apply for credit) will reflect these rejections. If there is anything that a subsequent credit reviewer does not want to see, it is that you have been turned down for credit in the past. Therefore, why risk the sophisticated credit analysts at department stores and the like when the local corner store, be it a grocery, five-and-dime, or what have you, will usually be more than willing to open an account for you? By keeping this account in good shape, you are automatically establishing a good, workable credit profile. This is the cornerstone of your pyramid upon which the rest of the structure can be securely built.

It is important to remember that stores make a great deal of money selling on credit. Even the major retailers want to give you credit if you look like you're a bankable risk. If you simply fill out the standard credit application and submit it, you will probably be turned down. Why? The store will check with a subscription service for your credit history and find none. Obviously, this is not the result you want your credit analyst to come up with.

Instead, you must play on the stores' desire to make a sale, enhance their friendly reputation, and reduce their risk when extending the credit. Go into a store and find something you would like to buy, like an inexpensive television set. Inform the salesperson that you want the set but have only half of the purchase price in cash and would like to open a charge account for the balance. Quite often the store will have a short form credit application at the cash register or will rush you through its credit department if one exists. If the clerk questions you as to why you want to open an account in this way, don't be afraid to tell the truth. Inform him that you have always lived on a cash basis, but decided it was time to establish a proper credit history. In this situation, the store has already made a profit on the sale in cash, and your appearance will be assurance that you are a low credit risk. You will have a store credit card usually before you leave.

You will also find it easy to get retailers' credit cards at busy times of the year. At Christmas time, or most holiday weekends, you will often see card tables set up with express credit card application service. In this circumstance, the store is boosting holiday sales by taking a risk of $100 (normally the credit limit on first issued cards) that you will be a good credit customer.

When the bill comes, do not pay it off in one installment. Instead, pay the minimum amount each month and be sure that you are on time. People often think credit is established if a bill is paid off completely. This is totally wrong. Good credit histories are created by paying off a debt in installments. When the debt is paid off, charge more on the card and pay that off in installments as well. This shows the credit grantor that you are a stable and consistent patron who makes timely installment payments as required.

The Importance of the First Creditor

The first creditor is very important for it is he who gets you your first registry with a local credit reporting service. Companies like TRW and Trans Union Credit are in the business of selling information to creditors on potential credit customers. Their reports show how you pay your bills, your address, Social Security number, employment and any past credit history, as well as

PLEASE PRINT

NAME		DATE	CHECK CARD NO.
LAST	FIRST	MIDDLE	

HOME ADDRESS

STREET	CITY	STATE	ZIP CODE

HOME PHONE	PHONE LISTED IN NAME OF

BANK NAME	CHECKING ACCOUNT NO.
(YOUR BRANCH)	

BANK ADDRESS

STREET	CITY	STATE	ZIP CODE

WHERE EMPLOYED	HOW LONG

BUSINESS ADDRESS	BUSINESS PHONE
STREET CITY STATE ZIP CODE	

CREDIT REF.

CREDIT REF.

SEX	HEIGHT	WEIGHT	EYES	DATE OF BIRTH
SPOUSE	HEIGHT	WEIGHT	EYES	DATE OF BIRTH

DRIV. LIC. NO.	SIGNATURE
	(AS CHECK WILL BE SIGNED)
SPOUSE'S DRIV. LIC. NO.	SIGNATURE
	(AS CHECK WILL BE SIGNED)

☐ CHECK IF TWO CARDS DESIRED   APPROVED BY   DATE   19

· I/We hereby authorize _____ to furnish the
(Fill in the name of your bank)

with the information requested below concerning my/our checking account.

Please Print

Bank Address _____
(Your Branch)   Street   City   State   Zip Code

Checking Acct. No. _____ Date Acct. Opened _____

Name _____ Date _____ Signature _____

Spouse _____ Date _____ Signature _____

- - - - - - - - - - - - - **Below To Be Filled In By Bank** - - - - - - - - - - -

Regular deposits: Yes _____ No _____ (check one)

Frequency of NSF checks: _____ per month

Any history of irregularities in this account or others under this/these names?

_____

_____

_____

Date: _____ Verified by: _____
(Signature of bank clerk)

Application for a Check-Cashing Card

credit limits, but you are not listed with these services until you are reported as a credit account by one of their customers. Therefore, it is easy to see that your first bill paying performance with, for example, the corner store is of paramount importance. The store is going to report you to the credit service or services that it subscribes to and if you are timely with your installment payments, the credit manager can only report that you are indeed an excellent credit risk.

If you are functioning under an alternative I.D., the information you put down on your first credit application is very important, so you must be organized. The information on this first application effectively gives birth to that person in the credit service's computer bank. Any future creditors will call upon the service for information on you and will only rely on the information so provided in making a determination as to whether you are worthy of their credit. In other words, good reports build upon good reports, and bad reports build upon bad reports. It is therefore absolutely imperative that you start small, establish excellent credit, and build from there, for the small companies who are easily satisfied will turn in excellent credit reports on you which will later be utilized by credit giants such as MasterCard, Visa, and American Express.

Credit Reporting Services

As mentioned above, the first credit application feeds into the credit reporting computers certain information that others will later confirm. When you fill out a subsequent credit application, credit researchers do a "cross reference" on many things listed on the application. The items that are typically checked are the name, address, Social Security number, driver's license, date of birth, bank account, and employer. If the information does not correlate with the names and numbers previously supplied, the computer will reject the application. Also remember that some credit researchers can and do check with the local DMV to see if the numbers you supplied for the driver's license, vehicle registration, and any other requested information correlate. Unfortunately, most DMVs happily and promptly respond with this information.

As can be seen from this information, attention to detail and consistency is of paramount importance in initiating a good credit foundation.

The Point System

After an application for a credit card is submitted, the credit grantor looks for a certain level of "credit worthiness." Obviously, the more prestigious the credit card, the more difficult it is to achieve that level of credit worthiness. For this reason, each card has its own scoring system, but most use what is known as point scoring. This system grants points to various types of personal information included in the application. Credit scoring by the point system evaluates an applicant according to a total number of points earned. Like a school test, one needs a passing score in order to receive that company's credit. The services correctly or incorrectly feel that a passing score is predictive of the applicant's ability and willingness to pay his obligations in the future, based on his actions in the past. Proponents of this technique say that by making the application a standardized "numbers game," the applicant stands a better chance of getting a fair shake from whomever might be reviewing the paperwork. What the analyst works with then is a final, total score. All of the characteristics included in the basic formula contribute to the score so that the decision is a result of a combination of weighted variables.

The following is an example of points assigned to the various factors on a person's credit rating schedule:

QUALIFICATIONS   POINTS

Telephone in Home 2
Dependents
     None 0
     1-2 2
     3 or more 1
Married 2
Single 1
Divorced 1
Widowed 1
Age Group
     18-23 1
     24-60 2
     Over 60 1
Years at Present Residence
     Up to 4 years 1
     Over 4 years 2
Checking or Savings Account 2
Loan Experience
     At bank where you apply for credit 5
     At another bank 3
Type of work
     Professional 4
     Skilled Worker 3
     Blue Collar 2
     Unemployed 1
Monthly Obligations
     Less than $750 2
     Over $750 1

Spouse Employed 2
Years at Present Job
    Less than 1 1
    1-3 2
    4-7 3
    8-10 4
    Over 10 5

The point list is indicative of one recently used by a major credit card company headquartered in San Francisco. But again the catch is the economic times. This is the variable that you can't control, but must take advantage of so that it does not trip you up when you are trying to sprint from the starting gate. Other factors that impact upon the score include salary, savings account history, and previous credit experience.

What is important about the point list is to learn what it is that the credit grantors are looking for and the relative weights they assign to each category. What you as the credit applicant are trying to achieve is an "aura of stability." You are trying to convince them that you are the kind of person that they can trust with what is in effect their money. You are trying to convince them that based upon your record of good experiences in the past, they can count on good experiences with you in the future. And, like anything else, there are a number of special factors which promote this "aura" of respectability. But in a nutshell, the basic rule is that the longer you consistently hold onto anything that makes you look stable, the better.

Beating the Point System

Once the theory and application of the point system, or any other system used by creditors, is fully understood, it is easy to work with and even around when applying for credit under a new I.D. As was discussed earlier in this chapter, each creditor looks at and weighs much the same information but qualifies the applicant in a different manner. The simple application of information contained throughout the book in conjunction with your own ideas is the best way to manipulate the system. Remember, it is easier to float with the tide than to swim against it. Don't try to buck the system, it is bigger than you are. Instead, you can buck it by flowing with it, using it to your advantage, and in the end making it work for you by understanding its flaws. In fact, this is also the philosophical tenant behind many martial arts. In judo, the whole point is to use your opponent's force and thrust against him. Don't fight him, flow with him, and use his strength to your own advantage. The following is a short list of variables analyzed by most credit grantors. Remember, the point here is to utilize the preexisting rules to your best advantage:

Home Telephone—Answering services work for you and will answer and respond however you direct them. If you have listed a service number as your home, have the service, upon inquiry, confirm that it is your home number, as required. Services often answer on home numbers when the occupant is out.

Business Telephone—Good answering services will answer as if they are business receptionists. For example, if you have listed your employment as that of a doctor, have the service pick up as "doctor's office." If you have instructed a credit source to contact the accounting manager for a confirmation of salary, advise your answering service. They will work with you. In that way, if someone calls and asks for the accounting manager, the service can instruct that he is out of the office, and he will return the call. Then you can call the creditor back under the pretext of being the accounting manager.

Profession—As was indicated on the point list, the applicant's profession is important. Don't be afraid to make up a profession with an inflated salary. The combination of answering service and mailing address will make it appear that you are who you say you are. Perhaps the most important factor is the longer the work record, the better. As a note, there are certain jobs that normally do not have requisite job status, including actors, waitresses, domestic aides, manual laborers, and quite often the self-employed. Tradition has shown that these positions do not have the basic stability the credit grantors are looking for.

Business and Home Address—Mail services are applicable here. Remember, length of time is very important, so whatever you put on the first application, be consistent on the next one. The longer the period of occupancy at your address, the more your credit grantor will like it. He is not going to be impressed by the fact that you move every year into a bigger and more expensive condominium. What he is looking for is someone who is stable and stays put.

Spouse Employed—There is no reason not to invent a fictitious spouse if she or he earns money for the family. The spouse's employment can be confirmed in the same way yours can.

Savings Accounts—Anything in a savings account looks good, but try to keep the balance as high as possible as this weighs heavily on the applications. For these to have any effect, they should be of record for more than ninety days. Savers tend to be responsible debt repayers.

Checking Accounts—A good checking account record,

with few if any "bounced" checks, is very important.

Building the Pyramid

After obtaining the first credit card, the rest is easy, but patience is still important. Inquiries for credit are shown on the credit service's records. As a consequence, if you apply for many more cards all at one time, your good intentions and stability are called into question. As in sports, pacing yourself is the key. As a general rule, five or six inquiries from credit sources on your credit report within a six-month period brings you under scrutiny. They will obviously want to know why all of a sudden you are in need of so much credit.

As discussed, the first credit card should be used and paid back on a consistent schedule. Do not pay it off all at once, yet do not let the balance due get too close to your credit limit. If the limit is small, after three months, contact the store's credit department for an increase. This too can look good on your credit report, as it shows the next credit grantor that an account you already hold felt strongly enough about your stability that it was willing to increase its risk and increase your credit limit.

The next step involves going out for a competitor's card. For instance, if you have a card and good credit with department store "A," try to open an account with A's competitors. Play on their sense of competition! The second card is not guaranteed, so it might be a good idea to do the part cash purchase and part charge technique used with card number one. Establish a good credit record with this store also.

I would probably then apply for another more exclusive department store card and upon receipt, apply for a gas company credit card. Then establish a good credit record on all. Please remember not to bite off more than you can chew at one time. It does no good to have a card in your wallet that you cannot use because you don't have the available funds to pay off the installments. Merely having a card does not establish a good credit record, but having, using, and thereafter paying back the debts established on a card will assure you of a superlative credit record. Again, go slow, be patient, and realize that you are building a major structure, not a small shack. Think accordingly, and you will not fail.

After approximately one year of slow, patient, and successful credit building, you are ready to take a swing at the majors. First, try the companies that are more aggressive, because of their limited circulation. I have always found that Diner's Club and Carte Blanche are good examples. The next step of course would be VISA and MasterCard. These companies scrutinize applications more fully than the others. But remember, a good credit foundation has been laid, and we understand what they are looking for. American Express is the most selective, but it is not that much harder than the other majors, assuming you can satisfy their particular requirements, especially the minimum salary requirement.

If You Are Turned Down

If you are turned down for a credit card, it is often because the company is being restrictive in its policies and its required point totals are very high. This is particularly true of the majors. Due to the government's "Fair Credit Reporting Act," upon your request, the rejecting company must explain why you were turned down. The standard rejection notice has a number that you can call for this explanation. Rejected applicants rarely call the company because they are intimidated and are reluctant to discuss their rejection with the voice over the phone. When they do call, it's normally to scream profanities at the poor clerk who is only doing her job in reviewing the application pursuant to company policy and procedure. Obviously, with what we have discussed in the past, it is clear that this is hardly a good technique.

You would be surprised at how successful pleasant human contact with the poor clerk can be. First, explain laughingly that you have not called to yell or use profanity. This removes the defensive posture which these clerks, after hundreds of irate phone calls a day, must assume merely as a means of self defense. Explain that the purpose of your call is twofold. First, you still want their card and are inquiring because you thought there might be some mistake; second, if there is no mistake, you want to work with the company to rectify any weaknesses that they perceive so that you can be fortunate enough to carry their card. You might just be surprised! The credit appeals person will be so grateful that you are not breathing fire through the phone lines that she will go out of her way to help you. At that point, your application will either be re-reviewed and the credit issued, or at least you will get a full explanation of what was wrong with your application so that you won't repeat the same mistake again. Either way, you have made tremendous progress, merely by understanding human nature and putting yourself in the position of the person at the other end of the phone line. Again, don't be frustrated if you miss. Rejections are not fatal as long as you learn from them. The one thing you do want to avoid however is applying for numerous cards in a short period of time, as your credit record will show all of the credit card grantors making inquiries into your file. This, for whatever reason, does not look good to the credit grantors and should be avoided at all costs.

Grade "A" Credit with New I.D.—
The Short-Term Approach

What is now a well-documented, short-term credit building approach was actually created by a maverick West coast banker about forty years ago. Since that time, this method has been promoted not only in banking literature, but also many "underground" publications as a sure-fire means of building grade "A" credit. I don't want to lull you into a false sense of security, however. Again, any time you are applying for credit or loans, the economic conditions of the time will, to a great extend, determine availability. For this reason, you must analyze the economic conditions that surround not only you and your community, but also the banking industry and the nation in general.

Short-term credit is gained through a series of passbook bank loans. A passbook bank loan is one secured by a savings account for the same amount of money that has been loaned. For example, if you put $500 into a bank savings account and request an eighteen-month passbook loan for the same $500, the bank will use your savings account as collateral. What could be more satisfactory to a bank than to have 100 percent security on the money loaned? The reason they have 100 percent security is because you will not be able to withdraw the money from your savings account until the loan is paid back. However, many banks will allow you to withdraw amounts of collateral equal to repayment installments of the loan. For example, if you pay back $50 of your $500 loan, the bank will allow you to withdraw $50 of your collateral. However, even if this is not possible with your bank, once the loan is paid back, you can withdraw the money so you will not have lost anything and will have in fact gained a few points of interest on your savings.

In a nutshell, the procedure works like this. In Bank "A" establish a passbook loan using $300 to $500 as your savings account nest egg. Remember, you will never lose this money unless you default on the loan. Take the passbook loan funds and open up another savings account at Bank "B." Thereafter, establish another passbook loan, and take these funds to Bank "C" where you will also deposit them in a savings account, and shortly thereafter establish a passbook loan for an equivalent sum of money. You now have accumulated a rather tidy sum of money, while in reality, you have only $500, or whatever amount you choose, invested. As you service these loans as they come due, you are slowly building excellent credit. In fact, the repayment of bank loans is the best credit builder you can have in your credit file. So, just like with your credit cards, pay the loans off on a timely basis, and over a period of three months or so, you will have established a marvelous credit rating and will be ready to take on the more demanding credit card organizations.

In poor economic times, banks are restrictive in their lending practices, so you will have to do much more research as to what the banks are lending, and under what terms. The general rule is that newer banks with fewer branches are more aggressive in their lending practices. Obviously, they need the exposure and the business. In applying for loans, it is a good idea to implement intimidation techniques you came across in earlier chapters.

Conclusion

If credit cards were easy to get, everyone would have them. By following the basic rules in this chapter, rules that the average person has no comprehension of, obtaining credit cards under a new identity can be surprisingly simple. Organization, patience, and a modicum of creativity is all that is required. Once you understand the basic rules of the game, utilizing your own creativity will make you successful. As I have said before, imagination is the key. If you only do what everyone else has done before you, you can only fall into the same traps. One of the reasons why pro football coach George Allen has been so successful, according to coaches of opposing teams, is that he doesn't always follow the standard playbook. In other words, Allen is successful because he throws in plays that no one else has thought of. By doing this, he has become one of the most successful coaches in professional football today. You should follow George Allen's playbook. Be creative, don't be afraid to experiment, and after softening up the opposition with a few runs up the middle, go for the touchdown by doing an end run!

10. LOSING A PAST IDENTITY

My experience leads me to believe that new identities rarely fail but that the people behind them often do. Understanding this sentence is the key to understanding this chapter because it is applicable to every level of identity alteration from the most basic to the most sophisticated. If a person obtains a new driver's license to avoid tickets and carries it in the same wallet with his original driver's license, he has failed the new I.D. and will soon be discovered. Likewise, if a person changes his name to start a new life and avoid past obligations, yet leaves a mail forwarding address at his old home, he has failed and will eventually be caught. What this means, simply, is that a new identity in and of itself is totally innocuous and inanimate. Like a loaded pistol, it has no life of its own, but once placed in the hands of a human being, the inanimate object can become a dangerous or useful weapon.

There are two questions to ask yourself when considering losing a past identity. The first is how badly do you want or need to disappear? The second is how much would someone spend to try to locate you?

Let's say you have decided to set up a new identity and walk away from $20,000 in credit card bills and a $200-a-month alimony payment. How much would it be worth to find you? Believe it or not, very little to the creditors. Locating missing persons is very difficult and expensive because 95 percent of all investigators are incompetent, while the other 5 percent charge huge fees and are very busy. It is no secret that all investigators claim that they can locate missing persons. However, if you quizzed them further and asked just how many truly missing persons they have ever located, few would ever come up with a number on the positive side of the scale. In reality, most investigators have the idea that locating a missing person merely requires going to the local post office and obtaining a mail forwarding address under the Freedom of Information Act. Ask them to go much further than that and they have no idea how to proceed. Sure, most of them know to contact the DMV, and maybe check for the new telephone listings, but most fourth graders could figure that out, too.

So at this point, it boils down to competence and money. Most creditors are reluctant to spend additional sums of money to find a debtor who will probably end up being insolvent anyway. So after spending an initial sum, usually less than $1,000, most creditors simply stop looking because the results are economically unproductive. Besides, they can write off the bad debt from taxes and will end up probably making more than they lose anyway. What they will do, however, is insert negative credit information in the subject's file, which will effectively prevent him from ever getting credit in the area again. This is one of the reasons why people are interested in changing their identity, and it is not unusual for some people to have four or five different identities going at once while receiving excellent credit benefits under all names.

Some creditors never stop looking. Although most evidence suggests that D. B. Cooper died in executing the first commercial airline hijacking, the government will not close his file. Why? Not only did he make off with $200,000, he showed the world how "easily" commercial airliners could be hijacked. I'm sure even Cooper would never have guessed that his original idea would become so popular and would result in every airport in the world looking like an armed fortress. The government investigators will never close the file until they are sure they can dance on Cooper's grave.

Another organization that has a reputation for never giving up a search is the mob. Why? If word ever got around that they were lax on collecting debts, everyone would be ripping off the greedy bastards! Even the U.S. government believes in the mob's tenacity. Their solution is to give gangsters who turn state's evidence a whole new set of I.D.

What these stories illustrate is that you must evaluate the circumstances under which you are operating when you make your decision to utilize a new identity. If one truly wants to disappear, one must set up a new I.D. and frustrate any attempts to be located. This for the most part involves severing the old identity from the new one.

How an Investigator Might Find You

I quite readily admit that I am rather immodest when it comes to discussing my skills as a private investigator. When it comes to the subject of locating missing persons, my bragging puts even Mohammed Ali to shame. However, like Ali said, "If you can do it, it ain't bragging." There are a few great missing person locators in the world today, but when they want and can afford the best, people come to me.

The one thing that I have found in spending years tracing missing persons is that people are creatures of habit and most are reluctant to leave something behind. By this I don't mean the bicycle in the garage, or the

bowling ball in the hall closet. What I am saying is that
after spending years and years of doing a particular
thing in a particular way, a person will find that it is
very difficult, if not impossible, to divorce himself from
that habit. While a person may be successful in severing
many or most of these ties, I have never found anyone
who could completely eliminate all of his psychological
and emotional links with the past. It's just too damn
comfortable to do things as you've always done them.

My favorite example is that of the young man, Chris-
topher Boyce, who was convicted of selling secrets to
the Soviet Union and sentenced to life imprisonment.
After he escaped from prison, government agencies were
successful in developing two leads which eventually
resulted in his recapture. Boyce was a known health
food enthusiast and a devoted advocate of the sport of
falconry. The FBI located Boyce in a small Oregon town
that was the mecca for people interested in hunting with
falcons. It was Boyce's past life that ruined his new,
peaceful existence in the Pacific Northwest. When they
put Boyce away this time, it is doubtful that he'll ever
see another bird much less a falcon, again.

If I were hired, with my usual, large, up-front re-
tainer, to look for a missing person, here are just some
of the examples of what could lead me to that person:
Friends or Family Members—Friends or family members
often know of the dreams of a missing person. They are
the ones who have heard the missing person speak of
"always wanting to see Australia." If friends or family
members were hiding this information, I would check
their phone bills for long distance calls. Other potential
sources for information of this sort are fellow workers.
Usually someone knows where a missing person is. With
this in mind, the good investigator realizes that what he
is looking for is not the missing person himself, as that

is too difficult, but that person who knows where the missing person is.

Previous Occupation—If a person's previous occupation was in any way unique, it can narrow the field. Professions often require state registration. I would check to see if information was forwarded somewhere else, or whether there has been any sort of name change on membership rolls. People frequently stay in contact with professional organizations or use them as references. I would also check to see if the person is qualified to do other, related jobs in the same field.

Hobbies—Hobbies are often unique and can direct an investigator to you. There are only so many places to surf, sail, ski, or hunt with falcons.

Prescription Drugs—People often take a drug or combination of drugs that are unique to a small percentage of the population. Pharmacies keep records and often the person's doctor is still contacted for renewal prescriptions. I always make it a point to ask my client whether the missing person has any type of disease or illness that requires prescription medicine.

School Records—If a missing person has taken the children, school records are frequently forwarded to a new location for re-enrollment.

Credit Records—While people may leave bad credit behind, they often take good credit with them. Reference will often be made to previous good utility records, phone records, and the like for new start-up service so that a deposit will not have to be made. People can also include some old credit information on new applications. Credit service files can be "red flagged" by investigators to see if past information has been retrieved for some purpose.

Government Rolls—Unemployment offices, Social Security offices, welfare, and worker's compensation rolls are often ties that people do not sever for financial reasons.

Asset Check—People wiring money from one account to another can easily be traced. Cars and other hard assets are frequently kept by the individual, but he makes arrangements so that the title is transferred into a new name.

Name Connections—People frequently change to a name they know or like. They will drop their last name and use their middle name, or keep their first name and take on the surname of someone they admire. An example that comes to mind is poet and singer Bob Dylan, who was born Bob Zimmerman, and who as a young boy, admired the English poet Dylan Thomas.

Local Contacts—Missing persons have been known to simply move to another part of the city in which they live. In this case, they will return to a favorite mechanic, store, or bar.

Habits—Habits are often unique. People are discovered because they favor one special type of shoe or dress in a certain way. People shop at particular stores, eat and drink at particular establishments, favor certain kinds of travel over others, etcetera. There is always something that distinguishes an individual that provides clues to his whereabouts.

While this list is not exhaustive, it serves to show how easily your past connections and individual qualities can make you traceable. Recognizing that you are more unique than you ever thought is the key to becoming untraceable. One must objectively analyze habits, local ties, hobbies, and anything else that can lead a trail to the new you. If you can successfully sever all these ties, no one, and I mean no one, will be able to find you. However as we will see, even if you can't sever a particular tie, you can at least frustrate the most professional investigator.

Creating Dead Ends

If someone is looking for you, two things can happen. He can either find you or run out of time and money and give up. Obviously for you, the latter is preferable. For someone to get within breathing distance of your new identity, he must first pick up the scent of the old one. Only then can an investigator find the jumping off point and start to locate the new person. The following section suggests just a few choice ideas that will frustrate an investigation. Again, these are only a few of the myriad of potential examples. The point is that it is up to you to be creative. The caveat that I have set forth throughout this book applies here as well: *use your imagination!*

One of my favorite tricks, although it is a bit morbid, is to have a client file a death certificate. Death certificates are filed by hospitals, mortuaries, relatives, and sometimes even the city in which the subject died. All that must be done is to find out how your local area requires these certificates be prepared and filed, and then do it yourself even if it has to be done under pretext. A nice addition to this is to file a petition for probate of the decedent's will. This starts the legal proceedings for dividing up your estate, which if you are smart, will have been removed long before the proceedings begin. The net effect is that when the investigator looks through the civil indices in the local courthouses to determine what type of legal actions you have been involved in, as he will undoubtedly do, he will come across your name in the probate files. Thereafter he will obtain the file and find out that you have "died." Our happy little investigator, realizing that he has just earned a rather tidy fee for a small amount of work, will sprint back to his client with the bad news, thus ending the investigation.

One never wants to leave a trail unless it is the wrong trail. If an investigator can discover the time and place where a person actually dropped out, he at least has a place to start. The wrong trail never gets him to the starting line. Credit cards and hotel records leave a beautiful record of the wrong trail.

As an example, before assuming a new identity, leave a major credit card on the floor of a bus depot in some far away, strange city. You can be sure that it will get plenty of use. Then, fly to New York with another credit card, stay at a fine hotel, make some purchases, and then charge an airline ticket to the Bahamas. Check in at the airline counter, but do not get on the flight. It is important to book reservations on a flight that is not crowded so that your one empty seat will not stick out conspicuously. Thereafter, destroy the card and assume your new identity. What you have done is to create a trail that even a bumbling investigator can follow to nowhere. All an investigator would glean is that you have either left the country or taken up a curious nomadic life in various ghettos.

Last but not least, don't be afraid to change your looks. Hair color, facial hair, everything. To be truly undiscoverable you must change internally and externally.

Conclusion

It is not hard to see that by setting up a new identity and implementing the protective measures in this chapter, as well as those which you will undoubtedly think of, it is possible to literally fall off the face of the earth.

All one needs do is to combine the factors of creativity and desire. It takes strength to be sure. Don't bet that the line won't be tapped when you call your mom on Mother's Day to tell her that you are all right and not to worry about you. Don't bet that some investigators, like myself, won't use every dirty trick in the book, and some that aren't. Some of us have read George Allen's playbook, too!

11. CONCLUSION

People often save the best for last. In this instance, I am going to share one final thought that the great majority of people never learn. The point is that no one can be trusted, so you have to keep your big mouth shut. It is easy to say, but difficult to accomplish, and if not accomplished, will result in bitter, painful lessons.

My favorite real-life example is that of a poor southern California genius by the name of Stanley Mark Rifkin. In 1978, Rifkin was a computer programmer who ingeniously figured out how to gain access to and make computer transfers with, the Security Pacific National Bank's money. Before the bank ever knew that $10.2 million was missing, Rifkin was in Europe and had purchased $8 million worth of untraceable gemstone diamonds from a Soviet broker. There were over 115,000 stones, none of which was over two carats. He pulled off the true crime of the century before anyone even knew the money was gone.

But Rifkin's perfect crime had one truly fatal flaw, and that was simply his ego. As a shy boy, he grew up in the shadow of those who were bigger, stronger, and better looking. This had become a thorn in his side, and the fact that he was now sitting on millions of dollars which he had accumulated virtually overnight, compelled him to show his genius to the world, including those who had snubbed him in the past.

Rifkin returned to the United States with the diamonds, checked into a fancy Beverly Hills hotel, and invited his attorney to his suite. He was just bursting to tell someone about this great scam and figured he could trust his friend and attorney. Unfortunately for him, he couldn't. Rifkin is now behind bars at Terminal Island, California.

I think this true story epitomizes the value of keeping one's mouth closed and shows what blind trust will bring. Don't let your ego get in the way of your brain. Let your ego be massaged not by the fact that other people are looking upon you with awe at the great adventure story you're telling them, but simply by knowing within your own heart that you have done what millions of others have only dreamed about, and have done it successfully.

I have now imparted to you the information you need to establish a new identity in America, one of the few countries in the world today where freedom can still be within your grasp. However, while I have entrusted these valuable lessons for your consideration, I leave it to you to determine if and how you will go about implementing what you have learned. I want you to remember always that my name is in the phone books in cities all over the country and throughout many nations of the world. Should you ever decide to leave one of my clients "holding the bag," I will find you and find you quickly. For while I have taught you everything you know, I haven't taught you everything that I know.